WONDERFUL

Wire

& Bead

CRAFTS

WONDERFUL

Wire & Bead

CRAFTS

Mickey Baskett

Sterling Publishing Co., Inc.
New York

Prolific Impressions Productions Staff

Editor: Mickey Baskett
Creative Design: Susan E. Mickey
Copy: Phyllis Mueller
Graphics: Dianne Miller, Karen Turpin
Photography: Jerry Mucklow
Styling: Kirsten Werner Jones
Administration: Jim Baskett

Library of Congress Cataloging-in-Publication Data Available

10 9 8 7 6 5 4 3 2 1

First paperback edition published in 2003 by
Sterling Publishing Company, Inc.
387 Park Avenue South, New York, NY 10016

Produced by Prolific Impressions, Inc.
160 South Candler St., Decatur, GA 30030

© 2001 by Prolific Impressions, Inc.

Distributed in Canada by Sterling Publishing
c/o Canadian Manda Group, One Atlantic Avenue, Suite 105
Toronto, Ontario, Canada M6K 3E7
Distributed in Great Britain by Chrysalis Books
64 Brewery Road, London N7 9NT
Distributed in Australia by Capricorn Link (Australia) Pty. Ltd.
P.O. Box 704, Windsor, NSW 2756 Australia

Printed in China
All rights reserved

Sterling ISBN 0-8069-5865-0 Hardcover
1-4027-0615-4 Paperback

Acknowledgements

Mickey Baskett thanks the following for their generous contributions:
The artists who contributed their talents to this book:
Marie Browning, Patty Cox, Caren Carr, Jennifer Jacob, Anne McCloskey, Pat McMahon, Vivian Peritts, Damema Spragens, Diana Thomas

For wire supplies:
Nasco Arts & Crafts
901 Janesville Avenue
P.O. Box 901
Fort Atkinson, WI 53538
920-563-2446

Artistic Wire
Elmhurst, IL 60125
www.artisticwire.com

For jigs & wire supplies:
Helwig Industries, LLC
P.O. Box 5306
Arlington, VA 22205
www.wigjig.com

For tiny holeless beads (Beedz) & Super Tacky Double-Stick tape:
Art Accents Inc.
4208 Meridian St.
Bellingham, WA 98226
www.artaccents.net

Table of Contents

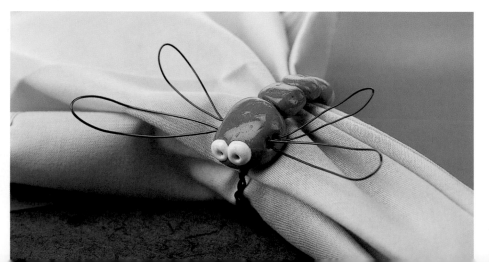

Wire and beads are natural provisions for a creative journey into the imagination.

Who can resist the beauty of beads and the colors, variety, and texture they provide? Who can resist the shimmer and gleam of wire? The sparkle and shine of both speak to our primal attraction to magical shimmer. The radiant glow of a beaded bracelet and the whimsical glimmer of a wire palm tree are only two examples from this collection of projects that draw us into the world of possibilities and showcase the versatility of wire and beads.

In this book, we explore the beautiful world of beads and wire with more than 50 projects for all tastes and levels of expertise – jewelry associated with healing properties, treasures and trinkets to give and save, and keepsakes and accessories to enhance your home's decor, including containers, candleholders, lampshades, and holiday decorations. Photographs, step-by-step instructions, numerous illustrations, and patterns are presented in the individual project instructions.

Don't resist the beauty of wire and beads – indulge and enjoy!

Mickey Baskett

All About Wire

Wire is the generic name given to pliable metallic strands that are made in a variety of thicknesses and lengths. Two basic characteristics distinguish one kind of wire from another: the type of metal used and the thickness, usually referred to as the gauge or diameter.

The type of metal a wire is made of gives the wire its color, and wire is often referred to by the names of three metallic "colors" – gold, silver, and copper. **Gold-colored wire** can be made of gold, brass, or bronze. **Silver-colored wire** can be made of silver, steel, aluminum, or tin-coated copper. **Copper-colored wire** is made of copper or copper plus another metal. The color of wire can be altered with spray paint, acrylic craft paint, or rub-on metallic wax. Wire also can be purchased in colors.

Commercially, wire is used to impart structure and conduct electricity, so it's not surprising that it is sold in hardware and building supply stores and electrical supply houses. You'll also find wire for sale in art supply stores, in crafts stores, and in stores that sell supplies for jewelry making, and from mail order catalogs.

Most any type of wire will work for the projects in this book. Just be sure to use the thickness of wire listed in the supplies to get the same results as shown. It is best to use a wire that is non-corrosive so that your projects will have a long life. Also consider the memory qualities of the wire you use. Some wire will keep it's shape better than others. For example, armature wire is very pliable and will not keep it's shape under pressure. If you are making a hanging candle holder, you will want a stiff wire that stays in the shape that it is bent.

TYPES OF WIRE

⑥ Armature Wire

A non-corrosive aluminum alloy wire, **armature wire** is easy to bend and doesn't tarnish. It is used by clay sculptors to build their armatures – the wire framework sculptures are built on. It is usually 1/8" or 1/4" thick or can be found by gauge measurement. You'll find it in stores that sell art and craft supplies. This is the wire that is used most for the projects in this book. This wire is great to use for projects where the wire is glued in place or wrapped around something stable.

Continued on next page

Armature wire

Buss wire

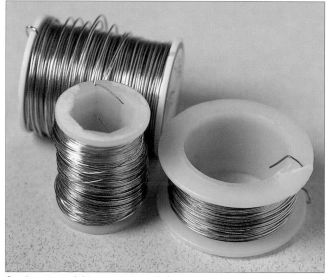

Beading wire and thin gauge wire and aluminum wire

Solder wire

Colored wire

⑥ Buss wire

Buss wire is tin-coated copper wire used as an uninsulated conductor of electricity. Shinier than aluminum wire and inexpensive, buss wire is silver in color and often used for making jewelry. It's available in various gauges. Look for it at hardware stores and electrical supply houses.

⑥ Aluminum Wire

Soft and flexible, **aluminum wire** is silver in color and has a dull finish. It won't rust and is often used for constructing electric fences. It's available at building supply and hardware stores, as well as many craft shops. It is a stiffer wire and will hold it's shape quite nicely

⑥ Solder Wire

Used by plumbers to solder pipe, **solder wire** is soft, silver-colored, and easy to bend. It comes on a spool and is sold by the pound. Be sure to buy solder that is solid core and lead-free. It can be found at hardware and building supply stores. This wire is also good to use for projects where the wire shapes will be glued onto something or wrapped around a stable surface.

⑥ Thin Gauge Wire

Bought by the spool or the package, thinner wire – from 16 to 28 gauge – can be made of a variety of metals, including sterling silver, brass, gold, copper, steel, and galvanized tin. You can find it in hobby shops, crafts stores, hardware stores, and stores that sell supplies for jewelry making.

⑥ Colored Wire

Colored wire is aluminum wire that has had color incorporated into the wire by a process known as anodizing. The colors are vibrant and permanent.

There are also metal wires coated with a thin layer of colored vinyl.

⑥ Beading Wire

Some wires are manufactured specifically for beading. Beaded jewelry is often made on a special plastic-coated wire that comes in a variety of thicknesses. It is sold in stores that sell jewelry-making supplies.

⑥ Wire Gauges

The higher the number of the gauge, the thinner the wire; e.g., 24 gauge wire is thinner than 16 gauge wire. The "Supplies" sections of the projects in this book list the type of metal and the thickness or gauge used.

⑥ Wire Mesh

This "wire cloth" is most commonly used for window screens and filters. It is available in aluminum, brass, bronze, and copper. It comes on rolls and is usually sold by the foot at hardware stores. The number of the mesh denotes the number of holes per inch. Wire mesh with high numbers is finer — almost like fabric — and is make of thinner wire.

Because of the popularity of using this product for arts and crafts, many craft shops now carry this wire mesh in pre-cut sizes. It is easily cut with scissors or snips.

All About Beads

Beads are made all over the world and can be found at crafts stores and the notions departments of variety and department stores. There are literally hundreds of shapes, sizes, and colors from which to choose. Beads are made of a variety of materials, including glass, wood, ceramic, metal, acrylic, semi-precious stones, and natural minerals. They are classified according to material, shape, and size. Most beads have holes in them for stringing or threading on wire. Their sizes generally are measured in millimeters (mm).

TYPES OF BEADS

◯ Bugle Beads

Bugle beads are tubular-shaped glass beads. They are most frequently seen in jewelry designs and beaded clothing.

◯ Seed Beads

Seed beads are small, rounded glass beads that are oblate in shape (fatter in diameter than they are long) and 15mm or smaller in size.

Various types of beads

Bugle beads

Seed beads

Holeless beads

○ Holeless Beads

Tiny holeless beads are exactly that. They add sparkle and shine to decorations and are great for covering surfaces. The tiny beads come in a variety of colors and are sold by the package, the jar, and the pound. They are attached with a special double-sticky tape.

○ Faceted Beads

Faceted beads are usually made of glass or plastic. They have flattened, reflective surfaces (facets) that are molded or cut, ground, and polished. These beads usually are transparent.

○ Stones, Cabochons, and Marbles

Stones and cabochons don't have holes for stringing or threading, so when used with wire, they are secured by wrapping with wire or gluing in place. Stones may be of glass, natural minerals, acrylic, or semi-precious stones and generally have irregular shapes. Cabochons are glass, acrylic, or semi-precious stones that are flat on one side, making them ideal for decorating flat surfaces. They can be tear-drop shaped, round, or oval. Also available are flat-backed marbles that can be glued or wired in place.

Faceted beads

Stones & cabochons

13

Tools & Equipment

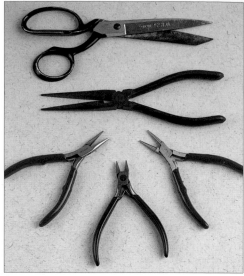
Scissors, pliers, wire cutters

✂ Pliers

Pliers are used for bending, twisting, looping, and coiling wire.
Jewelry making pliers are the best type to use when working with delicate projects and materials.

Roundnose pliers have rounded ends. Use smaller ones for delicate work and larger ones to make bigger loops.

Needlenose pliers or flatnose pliers, also called "snipe nose pliers," have flat inner surfaces and pointed ends.

✂ Cutters

Available in a wide range of sizes, wire cutters are tools used for cutting wire. Thicker, lower gauge wire requires sturdy cutters. Very thin wire can be cut with smaller jewelry-making wire cutters. Very thin wire can be cut with **scissors** or **nail clippers**, but cutting wire will dull these tools. Use **old scissors or metal shears** for cutting wire mesh.

Often pliers have a sharp edge that can be used for cutting wire. Use a **small file** for smoothing cut edges of wire or any rough spots.

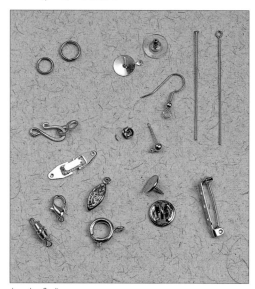
Jewelry findings

✂ Glues

Several types of glue are used in wire projects. When using glues, be cautious! Many glues emit fumes as they dry. Always read the label and follow manufacturer's precautions and instructions. Work in a ventilated area and avoid contact with your skin.

Jewelry glue is a clear-drying glue made specifically for gluing metal and stones. Find it at crafts stores and stores that sell jewelry-making supplies.

Metal glue is just that – a glue that's meant to adhere metal to metal. Find it at crafts and hardware stores.

Household cement is a general purpose cement sold under a variety of trade names. It can be used for metal, china, glass, and paper. It's available at crafts and hardware stores.

Epoxy comes in two containers – one contains a resin, the other a hardener. When mixed, their chemical action creates a strong, clear bond. You'll find epoxy at crafts and hardware stores.

Silicone Glue will hold metal to metal or beads to metal. It is thick and messy, so is better applied with a toothpick or other instrument rather than squeezing from tube directly onto object.

✂ Jewelry Findings

Findings are the metal items that transform wire and beads into jewelry. You will need the following:

Clasps: These come in a wide variety of shapes, sizes, and designs. Choose the type that you like the best. You will find *barrel clasps, spring lock clasps, toggle clasps,* and *fish hook/box clasps. Magnetic clasps* contain tiny magnets that hold together when they touch.

Continued on next page

Nylon hammer

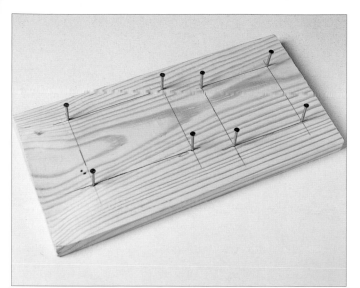

Home-made jig

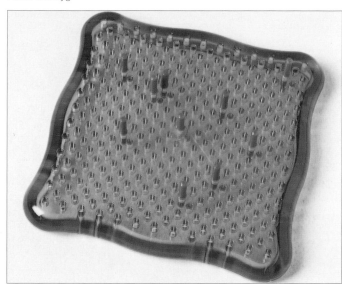

Purchased jig

Jump rings are small metal rings that are used to attach one finding to another such as to attach an eye pin to an earring back. They are split so that they can be pried open and shut for use.

Earring backs come in both pierced and unpierced varieties. Pierced backs fall into two categories: *hooks* and *posts*. Unpierced backs are available in *screw-on* and *clip-on*.

Stick pins and pin backs are attached to your jewelry design to transform it into a pin.

Headpins are earring findings used to construct drop earrings. They come in a variety of lengths. Beads are threaded onto the pin then attached to an earring back. The head pin looks like a straight pin without a point at the tip.

Eyepins have a loop on the end and are used in the same manner as headpins.

Crimp beads are used to secure the wire loops that connect fasteners or to permanently join two wires when you're not using a clasp (on a necklace that slips over the head, for example). They are made of very soft metal; squeeze them with pliers (crimp) when in position and they will be permanently shut.

✂ Jigs & Templates

Jigs are templates for bending and winding wire. Because some wires are not easily bent, using a jig to create wire shapes makes it easier to bend the wire into smooth shapes. Commercially available jigs usually are made of plastic and have movable pegs of various sizes and shapes for creating a variety of patterns. These are usually best for creating wire shapes jewelry or smaller projects.

For some projects that are larger and use stiffer and larger diameter wire, instructions are given for creating templates or making your own jigs from wood and dowels (or nails). To make a template, you'll need:

Tracing paper for tracing the pattern for the template.
Transfer paper and a stylus for transferring the pattern.
Piece of wood for the template surface.
Small headless nails (3/4" wire brads work well in most cases) *or* **small diameter dowels** for forming the wire. If you make a template using dowels, you'll also need a drill with a drill bit to make the holes for the dowels.

✂ Hammers

A **nylon-tipped hammer** or **rubber-tipped hammer** is used to pound wire to lengthen without changing the wire's round shape. A **household hammer** can be used to flatten wire. Be sure to work on a hard, protected surface, such as a stepping stone or brick.

✂ Protective Gear

Wire can be sharp at the ends and could cause injury if caution is not used. For safety, wear **goggles** when nipping wire and **protective gloves** such as cotton or leather gardening gloves. ❑

General Instructions

The following techniques are used in some – but not all – of the projects. Most projects require that you merely bend and shape the wire. But the following techniques are handy to learn for all your wire creations.

Making a Perfectly Symmetrical Twist

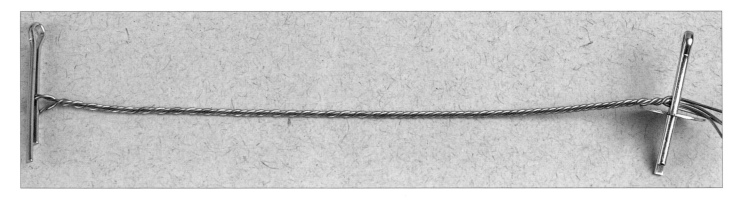

YOU'LL NEED:

2 cotter pins, 2" x 3/16"
1 fender washer, 1-1/4" x 3/16"
2 pieces, 16 gauge wire, each 24" long

HERE'S HOW:

1. Thread the wires through the eye of one cotter pin and fold wires in half at center around cotter pin. (Fig. 1)
2. Slide the cut ends between the arms of a second cotter pin. Hold ends of wires flat in cotter pin. Tighten the hold by sliding a fender washer on the end of the second cotter pin. (Fig. 1)
3. Slide folded ends down between arms of first cotter pin. (Fig. 2)
4. Holding a cotter pin in each hand, twist one pin toward you while twisting the other pin away from you to make a rope-like strand. (Fig. 2)
5. Remove pins from twisted wire. ❏

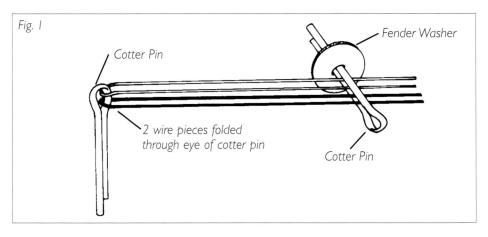

Fig. 1

Fender Washer

Cotter Pin

2 wire pieces folded through eye of cotter pin

Cotter Pin

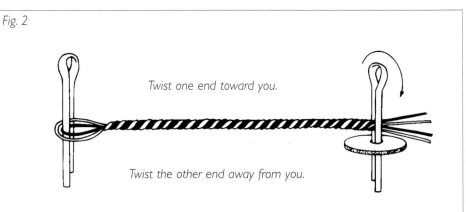

Fig. 2

Twist one end toward you.

Twist the other end away from you.

Constructing a Flat Coil Maker

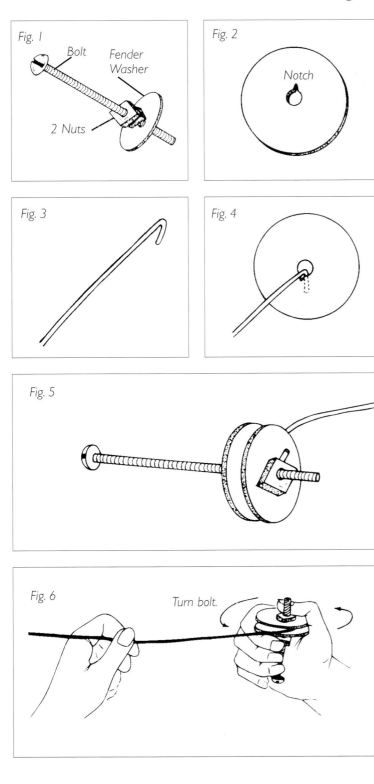

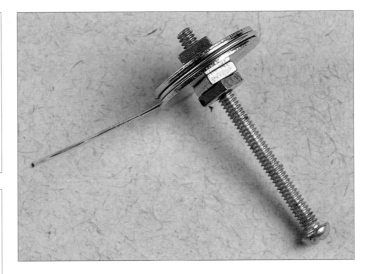

YOU'LL NEED:

1 threaded bolt, 2" x 3/16"
3 nuts, 3/16"
2 fender washers, 1-1/4" x 3/16"
16 gauge wire
File
Needlenose pliers

HERE'S HOW:

1. Screw two nuts on bolt about 3/4" from threaded end. Add one fender washer. (Fig. 1)
2. File a small notch on inside opening of other fender washer. (Fig. 2)
3. Make a 30 degree bend in wire 3/16" from the end. (Fig. 3)
4. Hook bend in wire in notch of fender washer. (Fig. 4)
5. Slide notched fender washer on bolt next to first fender washer, with the wire length between the washers. The bent tip of the wire should be on outside of washers. Screw remaining nut tightly against second washer. (Fig. 5)
6. Hold stem of bolt in fingers of one hand with thumb on top of fender washer near the threaded end. Hold length of wire in other hand. Turn bolt to form a flat coil of wire between the washers. Press top of washer with thumb while turning to open coiling side of washers. (Fig. 6)
7. When wire coil reaches desired size or the edge of the washer, unscrew bolt from end. Remove washer and coil from bolt.
8. Trim starting bend in wire with cutting edge of needlenose pliers. ❑

Making Wire Wraps

Many projects in this book employ the technique of wrapping thicker wire with thinner wire to secure ends of wire pieces and to hold pieces of projects together. Use 24 gauge or 28 gauge wire for making the wraps.

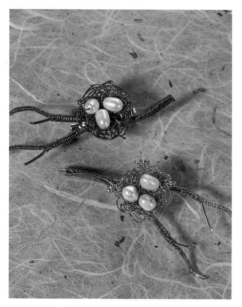

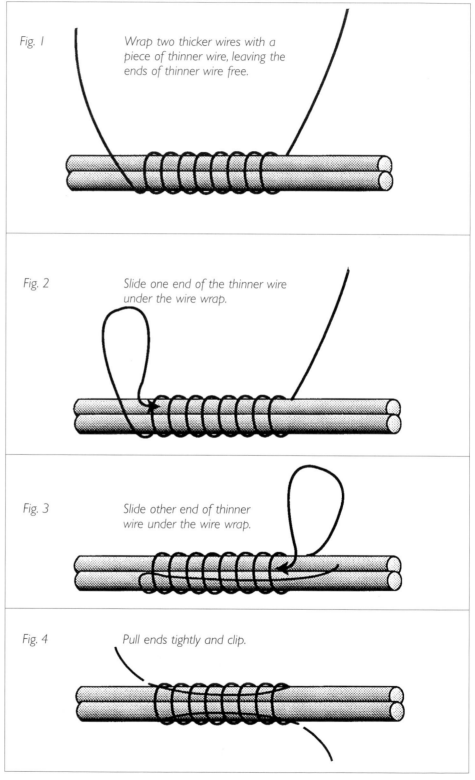

Fig. 1   *Wrap two thicker wires with a piece of thinner wire, leaving the ends of thinner wire free.*

Fig. 2   *Slide one end of the thinner wire under the wire wrap.*

Fig. 3   *Slide other end of thinner wire under the wire wrap.*

Fig. 4   *Pull ends tightly and clip.*

The Projects

The projects in this book show just how versatile wire and beads can be – for jewelry and for your workspace, kitchen, bath, and garden. You'll find decorative items and functional ones – and many that are both decorative *and* functional.

Each project includes a list of the supplies you'll need and step-by-step instructions. Many projects include illustrations to guide you, as well as patterns. Enjoy!

Categories of Projects

Healing Beads - jewelry that has healing powers
Wearable Wire - beautiful and whimsical jewelry
Notes & Letters - items to hold your correspondence
Photos & Memories - frames and other ways to display your photos
Garden Party - projects for outdoors
Kitchen & Bath - useful household projects
Around the House - from lamps to storage
Holidays - tree decorations and more

Healing Beads

Beads and semi-precious stones have been used for centuries as talismans and ritual objects because they are believed to possess powerful healing characteristics and to produce particular spiritual effects. Listed below are the birthstones designated for the months of the year and characteristics attributed to them. When you use these stones in your projects, see if you perceive their powers. Information on other stones used is provided with the individual project instructions.

Garnet	**Amethyst**	**Aquamarine**	**Diamond**
January	*February*	*March*	*April*
Inner fire	Intelligence	Soothing	Purity
Creativity	Brain power	Calming	Strength
Good luck	Cleansing	Safe water	Trust
		Travel	Commitment

Emerald	**Alexandrite**	**Ruby**	**Peridot**
May	*June*	*July*	*August*
Security in love	Regeneration	Stability	Warmth
Romance	Renewal	Loyalty	Friendliness
Joy	Grace	Royalty	Happiness
	Elegance	Beauty	Regeneration

Sapphire	**Opal**	**Topaz**	**Turquoise**
September	*October*	*November*	*December*
Anti-depressant	Inspiration	Energy	Communication
Protection	Clairvoyance	Protection	Serenity
Wisdom	Intensity	Warmth	Friendship
Creativity	Charisma	Balance	Connectivity

Color Attributes

Specific characteristics are also attributed to various colors of stones:

Black - grief, endurance, depth
Light blue - intelligence
Royal blue - love, wisdom, courage
Clear (Transparent) - clairvoyance, truth
Gray - modesty, obedience
Green (Emerald) - nobility, charity, understanding, temperance

Green (Jade) - power, fortune, justice
Orange - strength, abundance, regeneration
Pink - tenderness, affection
Purple - vision, intuition, chastity
Red (Ruby) - passion, warmth, devotion, tenderness
White - purity, peace
Yellow - faith, honor, knowledge

CARNELIAN & HONEY JADE JEWELRY

necklaces & wrap bracelet

Carnelian is the color of autumn and holds the healing powers of energy and physical strength. It is especially good for people who are absentminded and who need courage to grow and go forward. Jade, also used in these projects, is a stone used for protection.

The necklaces fasten with magnetic clasps. The bracelet has no clasp — simply loop it twice around your wrist — or make it long enough to fit over your head so you can wear it as a necklace. Adjust any of the lengths as needed to fit.

By Damema Spragens

Carnelian Wrap Bracelet

Pictured right

SUPPLIES

48 carnelian beads, 6mm
37 carnelian beads, 4mm
2 carnelian beads, 15mm
2 carnelian beads, 8mm
1 red jade fish bead
1 silver crimp bead
18" plastic coated beading wire, .018
   diameter

INSTRUCTIONS

1. Wrap one end of wire into a circle, using up to 2" of wire.
2. String on beads, following the sequence listed.
3. Unwrap end of wire and string on crimp bead. Place other end of wire through the crimp bead going the opposite direction. Pull both wires. Bracelet should tighten. Crimp the bead.
4. Cut off excess wire, leaving 1/8" to be woven into the beads.
5. Weave wire ends through beads. ❏

See instructions for necklaces on page 24

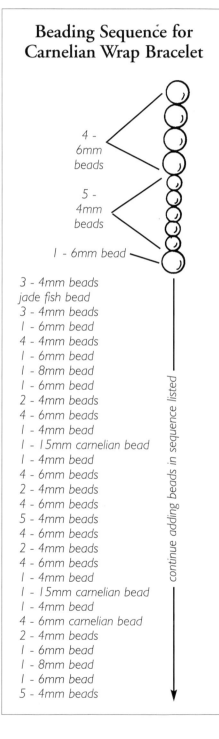

Beading Sequence for Carnelian Wrap Bracelet

4 - 6mm beads
5 - 4mm beads
1 - 6mm bead
3 - 4mm beads
jade fish bead
3 - 4mm beads
1 - 6mm bead
4 - 4mm beads
1 - 6mm bead
1 - 8mm bead
1 - 6mm bead
2 - 4mm beads
4 - 6mm beads
1 - 4mm bead
1 - 15mm carnelian bead
1 - 4mm bead
4 - 6mm beads
2 - 4mm beads
4 - 6mm beads
5 - 4mm beads
4 - 6mm beads
2 - 4mm beads
4 - 6mm beads
1 - 4mm bead
1 - 15mm carnelian bead
1 - 4mm bead
4 - 6mm carnelian bead
2 - 4mm beads
1 - 6mm bead
1 - 8mm bead
1 - 6mm bead
5 - 4mm beads

continue adding beads in sequence listed

Carnelian Necklace with Scarab

Pictured left on page 23

SUPPLIES

1 16" strand 4mm carnelian beads
1 16" strand 6mm carnelian beads
6 8mm honey jade beads
1 cream glass scarab bead, 14mm
1 silver magnet clasp
4 silver crimp beads
18" plastic coated beading wire, .018 diameter

INSTRUCTIONS

1. Wrap one end of the wire into a circle, using up 2" of wire.
2. String on beads, following the sequence listed.
3. String on 2 silver crimp beads.
4. String on one side of the magnetic clasp.
5. Loop wire back through the 2 crimp beads and crimp the bead closest to the clasp, leaving the other bead un-crimped. Repeat with the other end of the wire.
6. Trim wires, leaving enough to weave through 3 or 4 beads.
7. Weave wire ends through beads. ❏

Carnelian Necklace with Carved Square

Pictured center on page 23

SUPPLIES

1 16" strand 4mm carnelian beads
1 16" strand 6mm carnelian beads
6 honey jade beads, 8mm
2 carnelian beads, 15mm
1 pink jade carved square, 1"
1 silver magnet clasp
4 silver crimp beads
18" plastic coated beading wire, .018 diameter

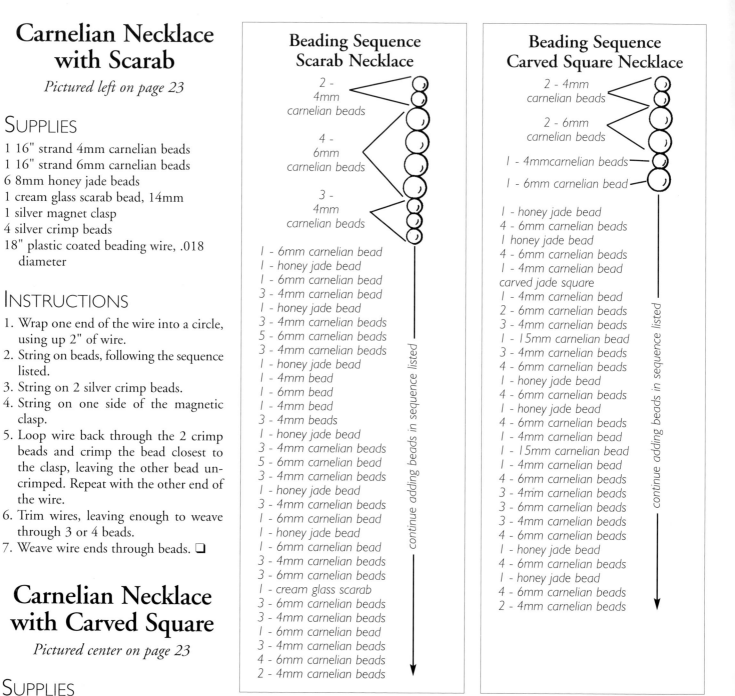

Beading Sequence Scarab Necklace

2 - 4mm carnelian beads
4 - 6mm carnelian beads
3 - 4mm carnelian beads

1 - 6mm carnelian bead
1 - honey jade bead
1 - 6mm carnelian bead
3 - 4mm carnelian bead
1 - honey jade bead
3 - 4mm carnelian beads
5 - 6mm carnelian beads
3 - 4mm carnelian beads
1 - honey jade bead
1 - 4mm bead
1 - 6mm bead
1 - 4mm bead
3 - 4mm beads
1 - honey jade bead
3 - 4mm carnelian beads
5 - 6mm carnelian bead
3 - 4mm carnelian beads
1 - honey jade bead
3 - 4mm carnelian beads
1 - 6mm carnelian bead
1 - honey jade bead
1 - 6mm carnelian bead
3 - 4mm carnelian beads
3 - 6mm carnelian beads
1 - cream glass scarab
3 - 6mm carnelian beads
3 - 4mm carnelian beads
1 - 6mm carnelian bead
3 - 4mm carnelian beads
4 - 6mm carnelian beads
2 - 4mm carnelian beads

continue adding beads in sequence listed

Beading Sequence Carved Square Necklace

2 - 4mm carnelian beads
2 - 6mm carnelian beads
1 - 4mm carnelian beads
1 - 6mm carnelian bead

1 - honey jade bead
4 - 6mm carnelian beads
1 honey jade bead
4 - 6mm carnelian beads
1 - 4mm carnelian bead
carved jade square
1 - 4mm carnelian bead
2 - 6mm carnelian beads
3 - 4mm carnelian beads
1 - 15mm carnelian bead
3 - 4mm carnelian beads
4 - 6mm carnelian beads
1 - honey jade bead
4 - 6mm carnelian beads
1 - honey jade bead
4 - 6mm carnelian beads
1 - 4mm carnelian bead
1 - 15mm carnelian bead
1 - 4mm carnelian bead
4 - 6mm carnelian beads
3 - 4mm carnelian beads
3 - 6mm carnelian beads
3 - 4mm carnelian beads
4 - 6mm carnelian beads
1 - honey jade bead
4 - 6mm carnelian beads
1 - honey jade bead
4 - 6mm carnelian beads
2 - 4mm carnelian beads

continue adding beads in sequence listed

INSTRUCTIONS

1. Wrap one end of the wire into a circle, using up 2" of wire.
2. String on beads, following the sequence listed.
3. String on 2 silver crimp beads.
4. String on one side of the magnetic clasp.
5. Loop wire back through the 2 crimp beads and crimp the bead closest to the clasp, leaving the other bead un-crimped. Repeat with the other end of the wire.
6. Trim wires, leaving enough to weave through 3 or 4 beads.
7. Weave wire ends through beads. ❏

JADE & JASPER

long necklace

Use jade to protect you when your life is in a state of upheaval or when you're moving.
Jasper is associated with contentment, compassion, and nurturing. This consoling stone
will help you nurture completion of projects and events in your life.

By Damema Spragens

SUPPLIES

1, 16" strand 6mm fancy jasper beads
11 fancy jasper beads, 4mm
5 hexagonal fancy jasper beads
17 fancy jasper beads, 10mm
1 carved green jade diamond bead,
   1-1-/2" long
38" plastic-covered beading wire,
   .018 diameter
3 silver crimp beads
Needlenose pliers
Wire cutters

INSTRUCTIONS

1. Twist wire in a circle, using 2" of wire.
2. String on beads randomly in a combi-
   nation that pleases you, using photo as
   a guide.
3. Unwrap end of wire and string on 3
   silver crimp beads. String other wire
   through the crimp beads in the opposite direction. Pull wires to tighten
   necklace. Crimp all 3 beads.
4. Leaving 1" of each wire to be woven
   into beads, cut off excess wire.
5. Weave wire ends into beads. ❑

IRIDESCENT AMETHYST

barrette & bracelet

The beads used here are purple glass. The color purple is associated with mysticism and intuition. You can substitute any color beads you wish that are the right size and shape.

Bracelet

By Pat McMahon

SUPPLIES

24 gauge copper wire
2 brass beads, 8mm
2 copper end caps
1 copper toggle clasp
21 coppery green iridescent beads, 6mm
40 purple iridescent bicone beads, 5mm
Needlenose pliers
Roundnose pliers
Wire cutters

INSTRUCTIONS

1. Cut 2 pieces of wire, each 10" long. Using roundnose pliers, fold one end of each piece over 1" from the end. (Fig. 1) Slide the attachment loop of the toggle ring over both pieces of wire (Fig. 2) and wrap the wire back around itself three times. (Fig. 3) Trim the loose ends with wire cutters.

2. Thread one end cap followed by one brass bead on both pieces of wire. Separate the 2 wire strands. (Fig. 4)

3. On one strand of wire, thread 1 coppery green bead followed by 2 purple beads. Repeat until you have used 11 coppery green beads and 18 purple ones. Fold the end of the wire over the last bead to hold the beads in place while you work on the other strand.

4. On the second strand, begin with 2 purple beads followed by 1 coppery

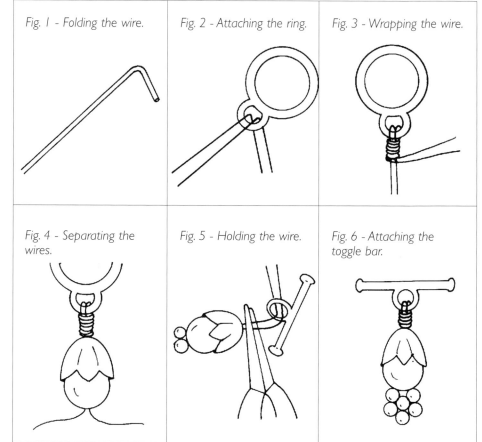

Fig. 1 - Folding the wire.

Fig. 2 - Attaching the ring.

Fig. 3 - Wrapping the wire.

Fig. 4 - Separating the wires.

Fig. 5 - Holding the wire.

Fig. 6 - Attaching the toggle bar.

green bead until you have 22 purple and 10 coppery green beads on the strand.

5. Holding the end beads – not the toggle – firmly, turn the two strands together seven times, twisting the beads around each other.

6. Thread the remaining brass bead on both wires, followed by the remaining end cap. Pull the wire strands until the smaller beads are snug against the brass bead and the end cap.

7. Using the needlenose pliers, hold the wire against the end cap. (Fig. 5) Fold the wires 1/2" from the end cap with roundnose pliers.

8. Thread the toggle bar on the wire end. Wrap the wire around itself back to the end cap, so there is 1/2" of twisted wire between the toggle and the end cap. (Fig. 6) Trim ends with wire cutters. ❑

Barrette

By Diana Thomas

SUPPLIES

5 yds. 28 gauge wire, violet
7 purple beads, 9mm
12 purple beads, 6mm
3" barrette with holes on ends
Wire cutters
Pliers

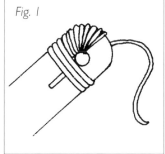

Fig. I

INSTRUCTIONS

1. Hold tip of wire along top of barrette and wrap three times to secure.
2. Wrap entire base of barrette tightly with wire, going through holes at either end. (Fig. 1) Leave 26" of wire at one end for attaching beads.
3. Thread 9mm bead on wire. Hold bead to top of barrette and wrap wire around bottom and back to top.
4. Thread 2 6mm beads on wire. Hold beads to top of barrette and wrap wire around bottom and back to top.
5. Repeat steps 3 and 4 five times.
6. Thread a 9mm bead on wire. Hold bead to top of barrette and wrap wire around bottom and back to top.
7. Wrap wire tightly around barrette between last 9mm bead and two 6mm beads.
8. Cut off excess wire and flatten end against barrette with pliers.

COSMIC POWER

three beaded bracelets

Let the colors of these bracelets mirror your moods (or lift your spirits and put you in a better one). They're easy to take on and off, thanks to the use of magnetic clasps. Choose colors that appeal to you, and adjust the length as needed to fit your wrists. These bracelets are 7" long.

By Damema Spragens

SUPPLIES

Colors given are for the bracelet shown at bottom of photo. Use colors of your choice to make variations as shown.

2 yds. 22 gauge copper wire
4 lime beads, 10mm
3 lavender beads, 8mm
7 orange beads, 8mm
7 fuchsia beads, 6mm
7 lavender beads, 4mm
5 lavender beads, 2mm
Magnetic clasp

INSTRUCTIONS

1. Cut four 11" pieces of wire.
2. Twist wires together for 2" from one end.
3. String a 4mm bead and a 6mm bead on separate wires.
4. String an 8mm bead on all four wires. Pull tight.
5. String on separate wires an 8mm bead, a 6mm bead, a 4mm bead and a 2mm bead.
6. String a 10mm bead on all 4 wires. Pull tight.
7. String on separate wires a 4mm bead and a 6mm bead. String an 8mm bead on 2 wires.
8. String an 8mm bead on 2 wires. String a 2mm bead on any wire.
9. String on a 10mm bead on all 4 wires. Pull tight.
10. Repeat steps #7,8,9 two more times.
11. Repeat step #5 once, varying the order of the beads. Add an 8mm bead.
12. Repeat step #3 & 4.
13. Twist wires together for 3/4".
14. String one side of the magnet clasp on one wire. Continue twisting wires for 1". Clip off excess and fold twisted wires to form a loop. Twist to secure.
15. Un-twist wires on the other end to 3/4" from beads.
16. String the other side of the magnet clasp on one wire. Continue twisting wires for 1". Clip off excess and fold twisted wires to form a loop. Twist to secure. ❑

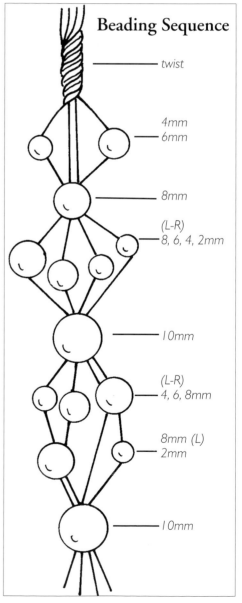

Beading Sequence

— twist

4mm
— 6mm

— 8mm

(L-R)
— 8, 6, 4, 2mm

— 10mm

(L-R)
— 4, 6, 8mm

8mm (L)
— 2mm

— 10mm

Wearable Wire

Wire and beads can be combined to create fabulous jewelry you'll be delighted to wear and give. The projects in this section showcase a variety of pieces – some bold and some delicate, some contemporary and some vintage-inspired.

Pictured at right: Double Coils Necklace & Earrings. See page 32 for instructions.

DOUBLE COILS

necklace & earrings

Thin gold wire is coiled into a tight spiral and then coiled again to make this mixed metal necklace and earring duo. Making the tiny coils is easy using an electric drill.

By Patty Cox

Earrings

SUPPLIES

16 gauge buss wire, 11" piece
24 gauge gold wire
1/8" armature wire, 6" piece
2 silver beads, 3/8"
1 pair earring backs
Jewelry glue
Needlenose pliers

INSTRUCTIONS

Make Coils:

1. Insert 11" piece buss wire and end of 24 gauge gold wire into drill. Allow spool of 24 gauge wire to drop. Secure wire ends in drill. (Fig. 1)
2. Switch drill speed to slow. Slowly run drill and pinch wires, allowing 24 gauge wire to coil around buss wire. Compress coiled wire tightly against drill. Continue coiling 24 gauge wire to end of 11" wire.
3. Remove coiled 24 gauge wire from buss wire. Cut an 11" piece of 24 gauge wire. Insert length through coil.
4. Wrap coiled wire around 6" piece of 1/8" wire. Compress new coiled shape. Remove from 1/8" wire.
5. Repeat for other earring.

Assemble:

1. Form coiled shapes into circles. Insert a piece of gold wire in each coil. Twist wire ends together to join.
2. Glue a 3/8" silver bead in center of coil with jewelry glue.
3. Glue coiled wire with bead on an earring back.
4. Repeat to make other earring. ❑

Necklace

SUPPLIES

16 gauge buss wire, 11" piece
24 gauge gold wire
1/8" armature wire, 6" piece
16 gauge gold wire
13 silver beads, 8mm
26 gold beads, 6mm
Necklace clasp
Roundnose pliers
Needlenose pliers
Beading thread and needle

INSTRUCTIONS

Make Gold Wire Beads:

1. Insert 11" piece buss wire and end of 24 gauge gold wire into drill. Allow spool of 24 gauge wire to drop. Secure wire ends in drill. (Fig. 1)
2. Switch drill speed to slow. Slowly run drill and pinch wires, allowing 24 gauge wire to coil around buss wire. Compress coiled wire tightly against drill. Continue coiling 24 gauge wire to a compressed length of 6".
3. Remove coil of 24 gauge wire from buss wire. Cut a 7" length of 16 gauge gold wire. Using a roundnose pliers, twist a round end in wire. Insert wire length through coil. Twist a round end in 7" wire to secure coil. (Fig. 2)
4. Wrap coiled wire around a length of 1/8" wire. Compress new coiled shape. Remove from 1/8" wire. This makes one bead. (Fig. 3)
5. Repeat the procedure to make 12 coiled beads.

Assemble:

1. Tie beading thread to one side of necklace clasp.
2. Thread a 6mm gold bead, a 3mm silver bead, a 6mm gold bead, and a coiled bead. Continue adding beads in this order until you have used all 12 coiled beads. Finish with a 6mm gold bead, a 13mm silver bead, a 6mm gold bead after the last coiled bead.
3. Tie beading thread to other side of clasp. ❑

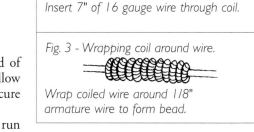

Fig. 1 - Drill and wire.
11" of 16 gauge buss wire

spool of 24 gauge wire

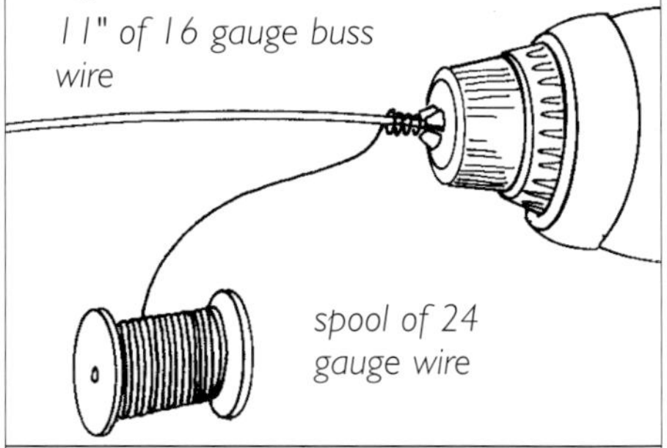

Fig. 2 - Inserting wire through coil.

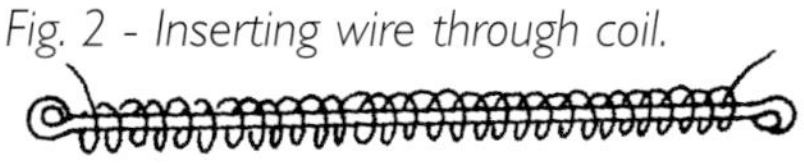

Insert 7" of 16 gauge wire through coil.

Fig. 3 - Wrapping coil around wire.

Wrap coiled wire around 1/8" armature wire to form bead.

BIRDS' NESTS

pins

Wire birds' nests on wrapped wire branches are wonderful resting places for these luminous pearl "eggs." The two brooches use different colors of wire. The silver brooch uses sterling silver wire, 24 gauge brass wire, and light blue freshwater pearls. The copper brooch uses various gauges of bare copper wire and white freshwater pearls.

By Marie Browning

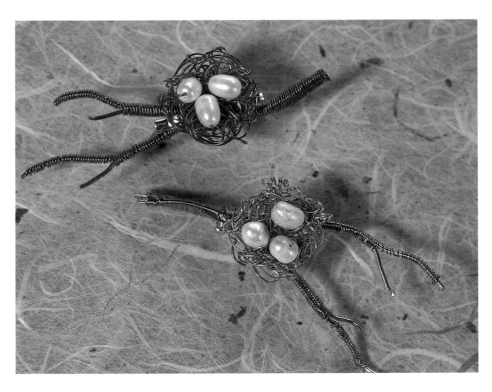

SUPPLIES

For one brooch:
1 ft. 20 gauge wire (for the branch)
24 gauge wire (to wrap around branch base)
20" of 24 gauge wire (for the nest)
3 freshwater pearls
Gold pin back, 1"
Wire cutters
Roundnose pliers

INSTRUCTIONS

1. Using 24 gauge wire, twist, coil, and form the wire into a nest 1" in diameter. Make sure the sharp ends of the wire are hidden on the inside of the branch. Bend the nest as you go, forming a hollow in the center. Set aside.

2. Cut 4 pieces, each 3" long of 20 gauge wire. Form the branch by wrapping the 20 gauge pieces of wire with 24 gauge wire. First, wrap 1-1/4" along the pieces. Divide the branch in half (two wire pieces) and continue wrapping for another 1-1/4". Divide the branch again and wrap the single piece for 1/2". See Fig. 1.

3. With a separate piece of 24 gauge wire, return to the first division of the branch. Leaving a 10" tail, wrap the branch for 1-1/4" around the two pieces, then for 1/2" around the remaining single piece of wire.

4. With the 10" tail, thread the nest on the branch and add the eggs in the nest. With the remaining wire, go through the nest several times so it is attached securely.

5. With another 10" piece of 24 gauge wire, securely wrap the branch to the pin back. ❏

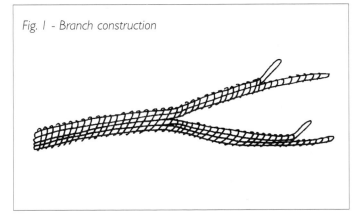

Fig. I - Branch construction

CONTEMPORARY DOLL

pin

Let this fun pin express how frazzled you feel some days! This is a somewhat large pin that looks great on jackets and purses.

By Anne McCloskey

SUPPLIES

20 gauge silver jewelry wire
Roll of sheet metal flashing
Round wooden disc, 1-1/2" diameter,
    3/16" thick
Metal pin back, 1-1/2"
Jewelry glue
Silver acrylic paint
Paint brush
Household scissors
Needlenose pliers
Small metal holepunch

INSTRUCTIONS

Make Arms:
1. Loop wire back and forth, forming a 5-strand piece 4-1/2" long with looped ends.(Fig. 1)
2. Wrap a small piece of wire tightly around ends of this piece, just above looped ends. (Fig. 1)

Make Legs:
1. Loop wire back and forth, forming a 5-strand piece 6" long with looped ends. (Fig. 2)
2. Flatten and bend end loops to form "shoes." Wrap a small piece of wire tightly around each "ankle." (Fig. 2)

Make Spine:
1. Loop wire back and forth, forming a 4-strand piece 3-1/2" long with looped ends. Cut.
2. Insert legs through bottom loops. (Fig. 3) Secure with wire wrap around spine just above the legs.

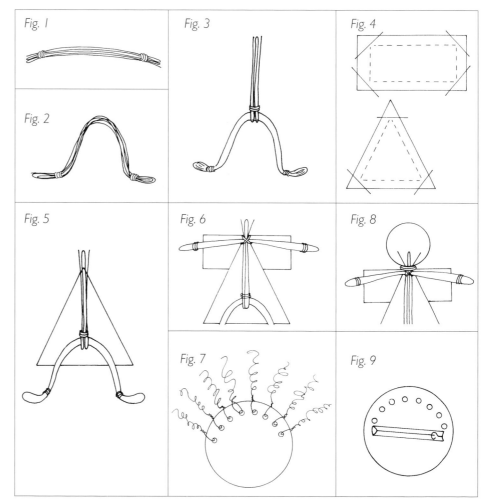

Fig. 1

Fig. 2

Fig. 3

Fig. 4

Fig. 5

Fig. 6

Fig. 7

Fig. 8

Fig. 9

3. Place arms horizontally 1" below top loops. Wrap with wire to secure.

Make Metal Dress:
1. Cut two pieces sheet metal: one rectangle 3" x 1-1/2" ("sleeves") and one triangle ("skirt") that is 4" at its base and 4" tall.
2. Cut across corners of triangle and rectangle. Fold edges under 3/8". Flatten. This will eliminate sharp edges. Add a bead of jewelry glue at back around sharp edge.

Attach Dress to Body:

1. Place sheet metal triangle right side down. Glue spine and legs to back, placing top of spine about 1/2" above top of triangle. Let dry. (Fig. 5)
2. Place sheet metal rectangle right side down. Position body (with triangle attached) so arms are sticking out of "sleeves." Glue in place. Let dry. (Fig. 6)
3. Decorate front of dress with coiled wire and small triangles cut from sheet metal. Glue in place.

Make Head & Hair:

1. Paint wooden disc with two coats silver paint, front and back. Let dry.

2. Punch 8 holes 1/8" apart around top edge of disc, about 1/8" from edge. (Fig. 7)
3. For hair, cut eight pieces of wire to various short lengths.
4. Insert one end of one piece through hole in head. Twist end to secure. Repeat with remaining wires, until all holes are filled. (Fig. 7)
5. Coil, crimp, and curl wires to form hair, using photo as a guide.

Make Face:

1. Coil short pieces of wire to make eyes.
2. Bend a short wire to form the nose.

3. Form an M-shape with a curved wire underneath for mouth.
4. Place pieces on head. Glue in place. Wipe away excess glue.

Attach Head:

1. Fan out wires at top of spine. Glue to back of head. (Fig. 8) Let dry.
2. Coil a piece of wire tightly around the neck. (Fig. 8) Glue and tuck ends.

Attach Pin Back:

Place doll face down. Position pin back on back of head. (Fig. 9) Glue in place. Let dry. ❑

DAISIES ON A CHAIN

headband, hatband, or necklace

This versatile piece uses green seed beads for leaves, white seed beads for the daisy petals, and large white beads for the flower centers. It is so pretty you will want to wear it all the time. Wear it as a necklace, or tie it around a hat as a hatband, or put it in your hair for a pretty headband.

By Damema Spragens

SUPPLIES

15 ft. 26 gauge copper wire
240 green translucent seed beads, size 11
130 pearl white seed beads, size 11
9 pearly white beads, 4mm
1 crimp bead
18" pale yellow satin ribbon, 1/8" wide
Needlenose pliers
Wire cutters

INSTRUCTIONS

1. Cut 2 strands of wire, each 5 ft. long. Twist wires together until you have 2" of twisted wire. Make a loop on the end and twist wires together. (See photo.)
2. On one wire (the one on the left), string 10 green seed beads. (Fig. 1) Make a small loop, placing ends of beads together and creating a leaf. Twist 4 to 6 times, creating a small stem.
3. Join with other wire and twist 4 to 5 times to create main stem. (Fig. 2)
4. String 10 leaf seed beads on other wire (the one on the right). (Fig. 2) Make small loop, placing ends of beads together to make a second leaf. Twist 4 to 6 times, creating a small stem.
5. Join the two wires and twist 7 times to continue main stem.
6. String 14 pearl white seed beads on left wire. (Fig. 3)
7. String a white 8mm bead on right wire. (Fig. 3)
8. Wrap left wire with seed beads around the 8mm bead, going underneath the right wire, creating the flower. Make sure seed beads create a full circle around the 8mm bead. Bend left (seed bead) wire across the top of the main stem. Pull it underneath the flower.
9. Twist the two wires together 7 times to continue forming the main stem.
10. Make more flowers and leaves, using photo as a guide for placement, until you've made nine flowers and 24 leaves and the piece measures 11" from first leaf to last leaf. There should be about 1" between each flower.
11. Twist main stem until it measures 2" from last leaf. Fold the end to make a loop. Slip crimp bead over loop and crimp. Wrap ends of wire around the main stem a couple of times. Cut off excess wire at end.
12. Cut ribbon in half so you have two 9" pieces. Knot ribbon through loops to create ties for the piece. ❑

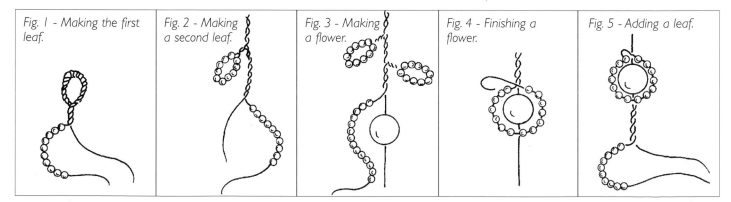

Fig. 1 - Making the first leaf.

Fig. 2 - Making a second leaf.

Fig. 3 - Making a flower.

Fig. 4 - Finishing a flower.

Fig. 5 - Adding a leaf.

Notes & Letters

The projects in this section include colorful accessories for your desk and decorative ideas for bringing whimsy to the workplace. There are greeting cards and pens in this section that will make your correspondence special.

Pictured at right: Safari Cards. See page 40 for instructions.

SAFARI ANIMALS

note cards

The leopard, elephant, and giraffe wire drawings are formed from bare copper wire and hammered flat. The designs are then stitched to black card stock and mounted on cards. Using a jig to form the wire is especially useful when you're making more than one of a design.

By Marie Browning

SUPPLIES

For the wire animals:
18 gauge copper wire (20" for each animal)
Hammer
Wire cutters
Roundnose pliers
Optional: Clear peg-style wire jig

For the cards:
Blank cards with matching envelopes, 5" x 7"
Black card stock
Animal print paper and/or handmade natural paper
Gold thread and needle
Tape
Glue stick
Gold gel pen

INSTRUCTIONS

Form the Animals:
1. For elephant and giraffe, cut one 20" piece copper wire per animal. For leopard, cut two 10" pieces copper wire.
2. Using the patterns as guides, coil and form the copper wire pieces. *Option:* Use a clear peg-type jig. Place the clear jig over the pattern, align the pegs with the turns in the design, and form the pieces with the wire.
3. With a hammer, flatten all the pieces. Re-adjust the shapes as necessary.

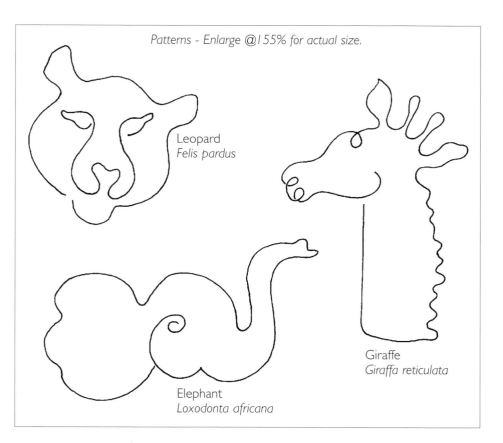

Patterns - Enlarge @155% for actual size.

Leopard
Felis pardus

Giraffe
Giraffa reticulata

Elephant
Loxodonta africana

Make the Cards:
1. Cut a piece of the black card stock to size (3-1/2" x 5" for the giraffe, 3-1/2" x 3-3/4" for the leopard, 5" x 3-1/2" for the elephant).
2. Sew the wire design to the black card stock with the needle and gold thread. Tape the start and end of the thread to the back of the card stock to hold securely.
3. Layer the animal print paper and/or torn pieces of handmade natural paper on the blank cards, using the photo as a guide. Glue the black card stock with the wire animal attached on top.
4. Add the animals' Latin names with a gel pen as a finishing touch. ❑

BEADED DAZZLERS

writing pens

Use these pens to add sparkle to your writing. They are easy to make with tiny holeless beads and double-sided super sticky tape – how the tape is wrapped determines the design.

By Jennifer Jacob

SUPPLIES

For each pen:
Round barreled ink pen
Double-sticky tape, 1/2" and 1/4" widths
Tiny holeless beads in 2 colors
2 box lids

INSTRUCTIONS

1. Wrap the 1/2" tape entirely around the pen. Be sure the tape is pressed flat, securely, against the pen. Remove the backing from the tape to expose the adhesive.
2. Wrap the 1/4" tape around the pen in a pattern – a spiral, a stripe, etc. Leave backing on this piece.
3. Pour one color of tiny beads in a box lid. Roll the pen in the beads until the tape is covered. Lift pen.
4. Pour second color of tiny beads in other box top. Remove the backing from the remaining tape. Roll the pen in the beads until the tape is covered. Lift pen. ❑

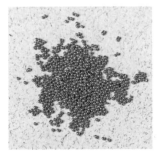

HELPING HANDS

office set

These quirky holders are great for memos, photos, reminders, and notes. Heavier wire – 18 gauge – in a variety of colors is used, and the finished pieces are pounded with a nylon-tipped hammer for extra strength. The paper clips are hand shapes with a coil in the palm. The file marker is a hand shape with a coiled stem. The memo holder has a face, two hands, and two feet held in a polymer clay base. It's easy to make multiples when you use a jig to form the wire.

By Marie Browning

SUPPLIES

18 gauge wire, copper and various colors
5 copper beads
Jewelry glue or other strong silicone glue
1 oz. copper polymer clay
Strong magnet, 1" diameter **or** circle of thin cork backing, 1-1/2" diameter
Wire cutters
Roundnose pliers
Ruler
Wooden skewer
Nylon-tipped hammer
Optional: Clear plastic peg-style jig
Optional: Coiled wire making tool

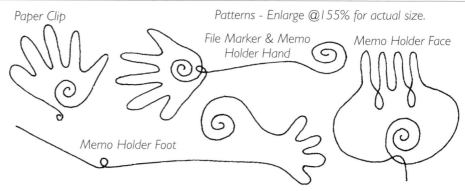

Paper Clip

Patterns - Enlarge @155% for actual size.

File Marker & Memo Holder Hand

Memo Holder Face

Memo Holder Foot

INSTRUCTIONS

Paper Clip & File Marker:

1. For the paper clip, cut one 14" piece of 18 gauge wire. For the file marker, cut one 20" piece of 18 gauge wire (5" is for the coiled stem).
2. Following the patterns, bend and form the colored and copper wire pieces. *Option:* Use a clear peg-type jig. Simply place the clear jig over the pattern, align the pegs with the turns in the design, and form the pieces with the wire.
3. With the nylon tipped hammer, strengthen all the pieces with a light pounding. This produces stronger pieces, and the wire stays round. Re-adjust the shapes as needed.

Memo Holder:

1. Cut 18 gauge wire in these pieces:
   Face - one 18" piece (2" is for the stem)
   Feet - two 20" pieces (5" of each is for the stem)
   Hands - two 18" pieces (5" of each is for the stem)
2. Following the pattern, bend and form the wire pieces. *Option:* Use a jig.
3. With the nylon tipped hammer, strengthen all the pieces with a light pounding. Re-adjust the shapes as needed. Set the pieces aside.
4. Make five coiled copper beads by wrapping 18 gauge wire tightly around a wooden skewer. Remove the wire coil from the skewer. Each bead is 10 coils formed into a round bead with the pliers. *Option:* Use a coiled wire-making tool – it's much easier and faster.
5. Make a coiled wire piece 5" long by wrapping 18 gauge wire around a pencil. *Option:* Use the coiled wire-making

tool with a larger diameter rod.
6. Condition the polymer clay according to package instructions. Form into a dome 1" thick and 1-1/2" in diameter.
7. Wrap the 5" coiled piece of wire around the base, pushing the coil into the clay to hold.
8. Push the coiled beads into the top of the clay base, using photo as a guide for placement.
9. Slip a copper bead on the stem end of the head, hands, and feet and place at the center of each coiled bead in the base.
10. Bake the base according to the clay manufacturer's instructions. Allow to cool. Test each piece to be sure it is securely adhered in the base. If loose, strengthen with a small drop of glue.
11. Glue the base to a cork circle 1-1/2" in diameter to protect your desktop. *Option:* Glue a strong circular magnet to the bottom to hold the memo holder on a metal file cabinet. ❏

Remember this stuff

Immediate!

Don't panic!

Right Here ↓

Pictured top to bottom: Memo Holder,
Paper Clips, File Markers

43

SMILING FACE

tile & tile stand

Keep this smiling tile on your desk – you're bound to smile back when you see it.

By Patty Cox

SUPPLIES

For Face Tile:
White ceramic tile, 4-1/4" square
2 blue half marbles
Solder wire
Jewelry glue
Toothpick

For Tile Stand:
1/8" armature wire, 18" long
Needlenose pliers
Ruler

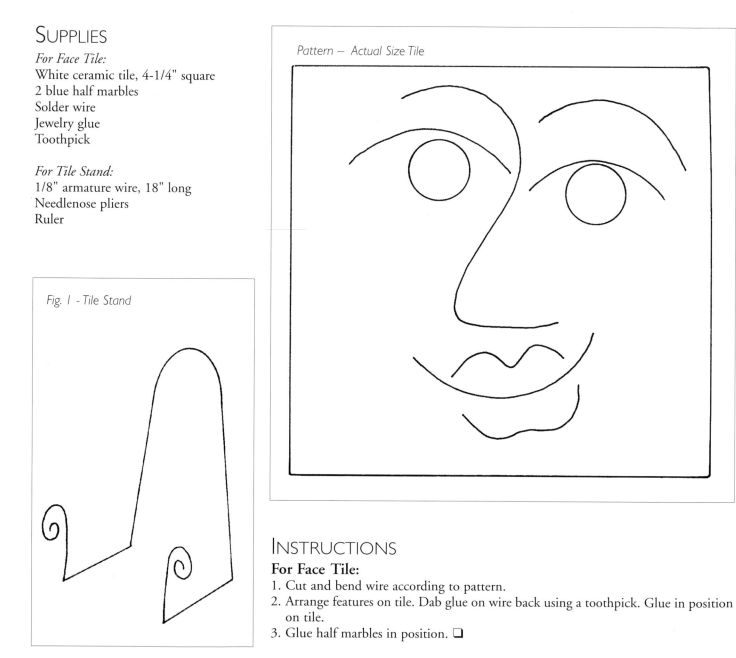

Pattern – Actual Size Tile

Fig. I - Tile Stand

INSTRUCTIONS

For Face Tile:
1. Cut and bend wire according to pattern.
2. Arrange features on tile. Dab glue on wire back using a toothpick. Glue in position on tile.
3. Glue half marbles in position. ❑

For Tile Stand:
(Fig. 1)
1. Bend 18" length wire in half to find center. Bend a 1" curve at center of wire top back of stand.
2. Bend wire at a 90-degree angle, 4" from each end.
3. Bend each wire end up at a 90-degree angle, 1-1/2" from each end.
4. Form a coil in each wire end with needlenose pliers. ❏

IMAGINE

tile with stand

Keep this sign on your desk as a reminder. The rough-textured clay paving brick is a nice contrast to the smooth, shiny wire.

By Patty Cox

SUPPLIES

For the Sign:
Paving brick, 8" x 3-5/8", 1/2" thick
Buss wire
Epoxy glue
Needlenose pliers

For the Stand:
Armature wire, 18" piece
Needlenose pliers

INSTRUCTIONS

The Sign:
1. Grasp end of wire with pliers. Form letters according to pattern.
2. Glue letters on paving brick using epoxy glue. Place a heavy book over wire until glue dries.

The Stand:
See Fig. 1.
1. Form a coil 3" in diameter for base back.
2. Bring wire forward, forming a lip for brick to rest upon.
3. Bend wire upward, bending end into a coil. ❏

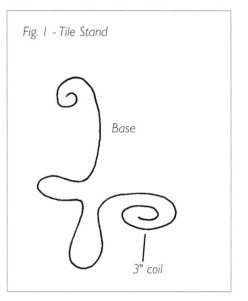

Fig. 1 - Tile Stand

Base

3" coil

Pattern – Actual Size

Photos & Memories

This section shows the creative ways wire can be put to use for holding notes and photos and memorabilia. They're easy to make and fun to share.

Pictured at right: Palm Tree Photo Holder. See page 50 for instructions.

PALM TREE

photo holder

This fanciful palm tree makes a great stand for holding photos, postcards, or reminders.
You could also use it as a fanciful centerpiece for your next summer outdoor party.

By Patty Cox

SUPPLIES

16 gauge buss wire
24 gauge gold wire
Needlenose pliers
5/8" spring tube bender (available in plumbing supply department of home improvement centers)
Vise clamp
16 oz. plastic disposable container
Masking tape or duct tape
Concrete mix
Pieces of sea glass or glass mosaic pieces
White sanded grout
White felt, 3-1/2" circle
Jewelry glue
White craft glue

INSTRUCTIONS

Secure Trunk in Base:

1. Cut a 1" hole in the bottom of plastic container. Insert spring tube bender with flanged end inside container. (Fig. 1)
2. Secure container, right side up and with spring tube bender hanging straight down. (We used a vise.)
3. Place a piece of tape over open end of spring tube bender to close end. (Fig. 1)
4. Mix concrete according to manufacturer's instructions and pour concrete into container, about 1" deep. Allow concrete to dry overnight.
5. Remove base and tree trunk from container. Set aside.

Make Fronds and Coils:

1. Cut buss wire into 24 pieces about 1 yard long.
2. Shape seven wires into palm fronds, using the pattern and Fig. 2 as a guide. Secure palm frond ends with a connecting wrap of 24 gauge wire.
3. Coil the ends of remaining 17 wires, using photo as a guide.

Assemble:

1. Mix concrete according to manufacturer's instructions.
2. Fill center of spring tube bender tree trunk with concrete mix. Insert wire palm fronds and coiled wires into trunk. Sponge away any overflowing concrete mix. Allow concrete to dry.
3. Glue sea glass pieces on trunk base with jewelry glue. Let dry.
4. Mix grout according to package instructions and apply over glass pieces. Sponge away excess. Let dry.
5. Glue the 3-1/2" felt circle on underside of base with white craft glue. Let dry. ❑

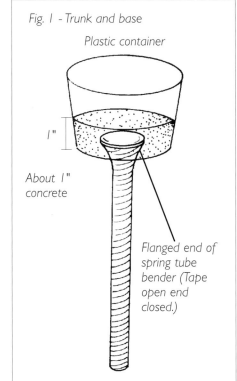

Fig. 1 - Trunk and base

Plastic container

1"

About 1" concrete

Flanged end of spring tube bender (Tape open end closed.)

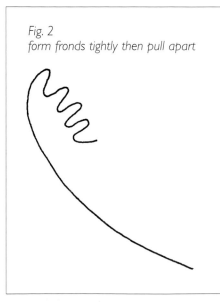

Fig. 2
form fronds tightly then pull apart

Palm Fronds Pattern — Actual Size

Secure with
connecting wrap of
24 gauge wire.

PRECIOUS KEEPSAKES

memory holder

A metal vent is used to make this handy holder. The vent's louvers are a great way to organize and display memorabilia. The coiled baling wire adds a great decorative touch.

By Vivian Peritts

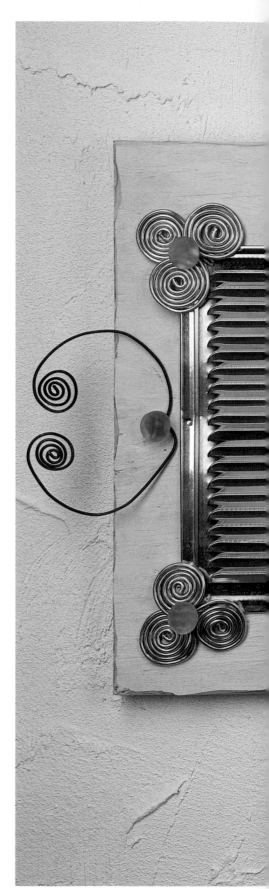

SUPPLIES

Silver-colored metal vent cover, 18" x 8"
122 ft. 14 gauge aluminum wire
15 ft. 16 gauge baling wire
12 frosted cabochons - 4 yellow, 4 blue, 4 orange
8 flower-top brass upholstery tacks
6 wood screws, 6 x 5/8"
Sawtooth hanger
Acrylic paint - off white
Paint brush
Rough-surface plywood or barn board, 3/4" thick, 12" x 19"
Jewelry glue
Needlenose pliers
Tack hammer

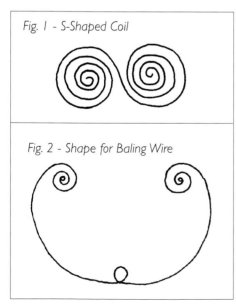

Fig. I - S-Shaped Coil

Fig. 2 - Shape for Baling Wire

INSTRUCTIONS

Assemble Base:

1. Thin acrylic paint with water to make a stain. Brush thinned paint over front and edges of wood. Let dry.
2. Screw the vent cover to the wood, placing as shown in photo.

Form & Attach Wire Pieces:

1. Cut six 24" pieces of 14 gauge wire. Coil all six pieces into s-shapes. (Fig. 1) Cut two of the s-shaped coils in half.
2. Glue one of the half-s pieces at each corner of the vent cover. Glue an s-shaped coil at each corner of the vent cover.
3. Glue a yellow cabochon at each corner where the coils meet.
4. Cut baling wire into eight 24" lengths. Coil the ends of each. (Fig. 2) Twist at center to make a small loop.
5. Position coiled baling wire on board as shown in photo (three at top and bottom, one at each side). Insert an upholstery tack through the loop of each wire coil. Press or hammer tacks in place.
6. Glue orange cabochons over the top center and bottom center tacks and the side tacks.
7. Glue blue cabochons over the remaining tacks.
8. Attach a sawtooth hanger to the back. ❑

COLORFUL COIL

picture frame

Beads on coiled armature wire add color and whimsy to an inexpensive plastic box frame. This one holds a vintage postcard.

By Patty Cox

SUPPLIES

1/8" armature wire
24 gauge gold wire
36 plastic beads to fit on armature wire, various colors
Clear plastic box frame, 3-1/2" x 5"
1/2" dowel
Needlenose pliers
Drill with 1/8" bit
Jewelry glue
Ruler
Waterbase fine-tip marker

INSTRUCTIONS

1. Draw a line around the sides of box frame, 1/2" from each edge. For hole placement, mark 1/8" from each end, and 3/8" apart.
2. Drill a hole at each mark.
3. Wrap armature wire in a spiral around a 1/2" dowel. Compress coil. Remove from dowel.
4. Gently pull coil apart, separating spirals about 3/8". Thread several pony beads on wire.
5. Place end of spiraled wire at center bottom of box frame. Attach each spiral to frame with a loop of 24 gauge wire by threading the 24 gauge wire through the inside of the frame, bring it out through a drilled hole, wrapping it around the armature wire spiral where the spiral touches the frame, and then threading the 24 gauge wire

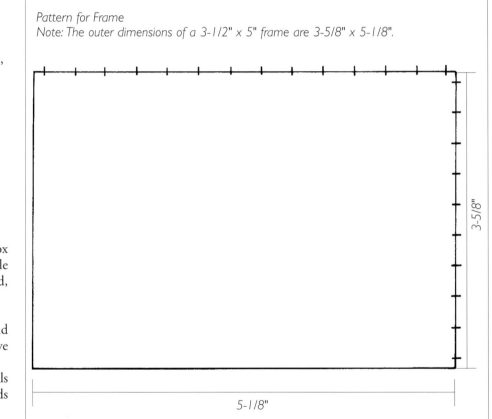

Pattern for Frame
Note: The outer dimensions of a 3-1/2" x 5" frame are 3-5/8" x 5-1/8".

3-5/8"

5-1/8"

back through same hole in box frame. Repeat this process to secure all the spirals with wire at the holes in the frame, placing a pony bead on every other spiral before attaching with 24 gauge wire.
6. Trim end of spiraled wire so it butts against the beginning of the spiraled wire. Finish wiring spiraled sections to the frame.
7. Secure pony beads with glue to keep them from slipping around. ❑

LEND A HAND

holder for jewelry, photos, or recipes

Put this handy holder to work for you on your desk, kitchen counter, or dresser.

By Patty Cox

SUPPLIES

1/8" armature wire
24 gauge gold wire
1/2" dowel
1/4" dowel or pencil
Needlenose pliers

INSTRUCTIONS

1. Cut 73" of armature wire. Leave a 16" tail, then begin to form the hand shape, starting with the little finger side.
2. Form the curves of the fingertips around a 1/2" dowel. Bend inside curves of fingers around a 1/4" dowel or pencil.
3. Bend the 5" at each end at a 90-degree angle. Curve the bent end pieces to form a circular stand 3-1/2" in diameter. Secure wire ends with connecting wraps of 24 gauge wire.
4. Cut two 12" pieces armature wire. Using the pattern provided, form each piece into an s-shape. Connect s-shapes at center to form a heart shape. Secure heart in palm of hand with connecting wraps of 24 gauge wire. ❏

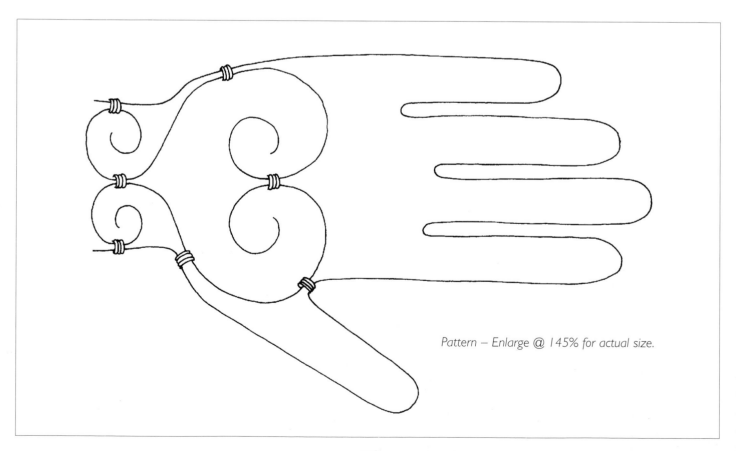

Pattern – Enlarge @ 145% for actual size.

GRAPE CLUSTERS

picture frame

Wire is used to form grapes, leaves, and tendrils that are mounted on
a simple wooden frame.

By Anne McCloskey

SUPPLIES

Several spools of 20 gauge gold beading
   wire
Wooden picture frame, 11" x 14"
Acrylic craft paint - black, metallic gold
   acrylic paints medium
Paint brushes
Jewelry glue
Pencil
Wire cutters
Sponge
Sandpaper
Needlenose pliers
Sawtooth hanger

INSTRUCTIONS

Paint Frame:
1. Lightly sand frame. Wipe away dust.
2. Paint front and sides of frame with black.
3. Dampen sponge and dip in gold
   paint. Wipe gold paint on frame to
   make streaks. Blend the two colors
   slightly to soften. Let dry.

Make Grapes:
*The technique for making the grapes is the
same for all of them; the sizes vary.*
1. Form a 1" circle of wire. Holding the
   spool, wrap around that shape several
   times one way, then reverse and wrap
   in another direction. Continue wrapping until you have formed a wire ball
   1" wide. Cut the end and tuck it into
   the ball.
2. Make 19 more grapes in five different
   sizes.
3. Arrange them to form a grape cluster
   on the frame as shown in the photo.

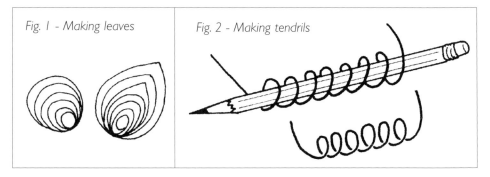

Fig. 1 - Making leaves   Fig. 2 - Making tendrils

Make Leaves:
You will make five leaves in several sizes.
1. Using pliers or your hands, coil three round loops that are fairly tight, then make
   four larger loops. (Fig. 1)
2. Pinch the four larger loops to form a leaf shape.
3. Cut a small piece of wire, pass it through the center coil, and twist the ends together
   to form a stem to hold the leaf together.
4. Make four more leaves.

Make Stems:
1. Cut eight 8" pieces of wire.
2. Fold wire pieces in half. Hold four pieces with folded ends together. Wrap with
   another piece of wire to form a stem. Cut wire and tuck end into the stem.
3. Make a second stem, repeating the process, with the remaining four wire pieces.

Make Tendrils:
1. Cut three pieces of wire 8" long. Wind the wire around a pencil in a spiral. Pull off.
   (Fig. 2)
2. Pull slightly to shape.

Assemble:
1. Twist the leaves, stem, and tendrils for one cluster together, adding wire as needed
   to secure. Do the same to leaves, stem, and tendrils of the other cluster.
2. Glue leaf clusters to the frame as shown in photo.
3. Arrange grape clusters on frame, using photo as a guide, gluing the larger grapes
   next to the stems, adding them one at a time. Let dry.
4. Be sure all the pieces are securely attached. Bend the leaves and tendrils as shown.
5. For aged look, dab a small amount of black paint on each grape and on the leaves,
   stems, and tendrils. ❏

Garden Party

Wire and beads go to the garden in this section, which includes imaginative table accessories for dining alfresco, plant pokes and garden ornaments, fabulous flowers that don't wilt, votive holders for lighting up the landscape, and a nature-inspired frame.

Pictured at right: Garden Critters Table Accessories. See page 62 for instructions.

GARDEN CRITTERS

table accessories

These cheerfully colored, sociable garden critters will brighten your backyard or patio table. The set includes a firefly candle companion, a dragonfly napkin holder, and snail place card and menu holders. You can also make the snails so they will hang from glasses or vases.

By Marie Browning

SUPPLIES

20 gauge colored wire - teal
Shells, one for each snail
4 colors polymer clay - green, teal, yellow, and white
Polymer clay varnish
Round wooden toothpick
Nylon tipped hammer
Wire cutters
Roundnose pliers
Ruler

INSTRUCTIONS

Form the Clay Pieces:

1. Condition the polymer clay according to the manufacturer's instructions.
2. Form and join the clay pieces that make up the critters, using the patterns provided.
3. With a wooden toothpick, make the holes in the middles of the white balls to create the eyes.

Cut & Form Wire:

With teal wire, form wings, legs, and antennae, using the patterns provided.

Construct the Firefly:

Push the ends of the antenna into the head, the heart shaped wings into the body, and the legs into the base of the body shape.

Continued on next page

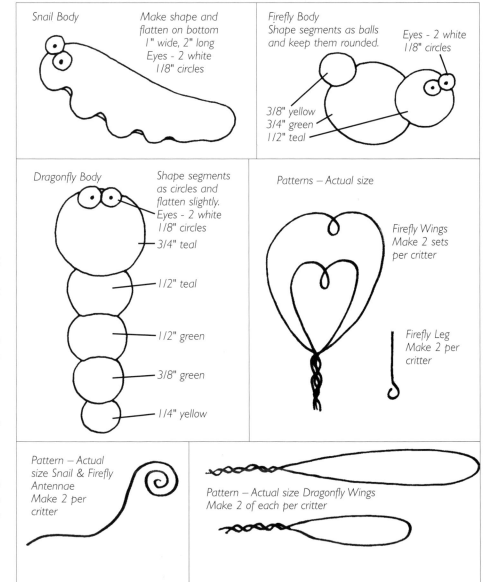

Snail Body
Make shape and flatten on bottom
1" wide, 2" long
Eyes - 2 white
1/8" circles

Firefly Body
Shape segments as balls and keep them rounded.
Eyes - 2 white
1/8" circles
3/8" yellow
3/4" green
1/2" teal

Dragonfly Body
Shape segments as circles and flatten slightly.
Eyes - 2 white
1/8" circles
3/4" teal
1/2" teal
1/2" green
3/8" green
1/4" yellow

Patterns – Actual size
Firefly Wings
Make 2 sets per critter
Firefly Leg
Make 2 per critter

Pattern – Actual size Snail & Firefly Antennae
Make 2 per critter

Pattern – Actual size Dragonfly Wings
Make 2 of each per critter

Construct the Snail:

Push the antennae into the top of the head and push a shell on the back of the body. **For flowerpot or glass "hangers":** Shape snails over clay pot rims.

Construct the Dragonfly Napkin Ring:

1. Cut two 6" pieces of teal wire. Fold each piece. Twist to form two two-strand twists.
2. Twist those two twists together to form a four-strand twisted piece. Form this into a circle 2" in diameter.
3. Place the polymer clay dragonfly body over the wire. Press a small, thin strip of polymer clay under the body to secure the dragonfly to the wire circle.
4. Place the dragonfly wings in the main body piece.

Finish:

1. Bake the critters, following the clay manufacturer's instructions. Let cool.
2. Brush with a coat of polymer clay varnish to finish. ❑

Pictured clockwise from top left: Snail, Dragonfly Napkin Ring, Firefly

AFRICAN VIOLETS

wire sculpture

Here's a potted plant that needs no upkeep other than an occasional dusting.

By Anne McCloskey

SUPPLIES

Paddle of medium gauge silver wire
Roll of aluminum sheet metal flashing
100 yellow beads, 3mm
Terra cotta pot, 5" diameter
Acrylic craft paint - dark green, white,
    medium green, lavender, rust, dark
    brown, black
Paint brush
Gloss varnish
Jewelry glue
White paper
Pencil
Double-sided masking tape
Paper towels
Small needlenose pliers
Household scissors
Tweezers
Metal hole punch
Plastic foam block

INSTRUCTIONS

Prepare:

1. Trace leaf and flower patterns on paper. Cut out.
2. Using a paper towel dampened with soap and water, clean metal flashing. Rinse and dry.
3. Tape patterns to the metal. Cut out 5 large and 3 small leaves. Cut out 3 large and 6 small flowers.

Make Flowers:

1. Punch a small hole through flower center with hole punch. Paint both sides of each flower with lavender. Let dry.
2. Varnish both sides of each flower. Let dry.
3. Gently bend flower petals toward center, cupping the flower into a natural shape.
4. With wire and pliers, create a small round coil to fit each petal. (There will be 5 coils per flower.) Apply a small amount of glue to the underside of each wire coil and press a coil on each petal. Wipe away excess glue. Let dry.
5. Place a small amount of glue in the center of one flower. Cut a 10" piece of wire. Coil one end into a flat circle. Insert the wire into the glued center with the coil inserted deep in the glue. With the tweezers, pick up the beads one at a time and place them into the glue, creating a mounded, clustered center. Let dry.

Make Leaves:

1. Cut a 12" piece of wire to make a stem for each leaf. Glue stem down the center front of leaf, with the wire hanging out the stem end. Let dry.
2. Gently bend each leaf toward its center, creating a dimensional look.
3. Paint each leaf with dark green paint down the leaf center. Double load white and medium green paint on the brush and stroke leaf from center to sides to create a striated effect. Let dry.
4. Stroke the dry brush down the center vein and from the sides to the center to create a veined look. Wipe off brush as needed. Complete all leaves. Let dry.

Continued on next page

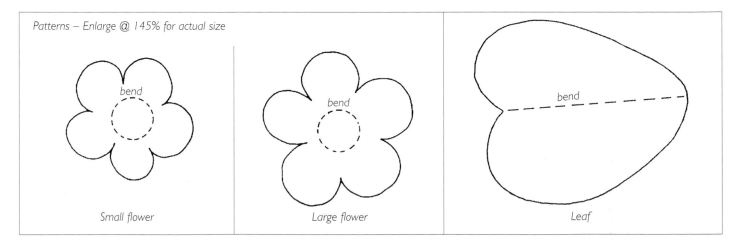

Patterns – Enlarge @ 145% for actual size

bend

bend

bend

Small flower   *Large flower*   *Leaf*

5. Apply varnish to tops of leaves. Let dry.
6. Turn leaves over. Paint undersides with dark green. Let dry.
7. Apply varnish to undersides and let dry.

Decorate the Pot:

1. Trace the pot's diameter on sheet metal. Cut out the metal circle. (It should just fit inside the pot.)
2. With the hole punch, make a 1/2" hole in the center of the metal circle.
3. Dab black and brown paint over the circle to resemble soil. Let dry.
4. Varnish over paint. Let dry.
5. Cut foam block to fit in pot. Place foam in pot, securing with glue. Apply glue to top of foam and firmly place the painted metal circle on top.
6. Lightly apply glue around sides of pot. Coil wire around pot as shown in photo. At the rim, bend wire in a series of loops all the way around the pot's circumference. Glue in place. Wipe away excess glue. Let dry.
7. Using a paper towel, gently smear a small amount of rust paint over the glued wire to give an aged appearance. Wipe away some of the paint.

Assemble:

1. Make an arrangement, clustering the larger leaves and twisting the stems together, then adding the smaller leaves on top and twisting their stems together.
2. Add the larger flowers, one at a time, twisting their stems into those of the leaves so they peek out from the leaves, here and there. Put the smaller flowers near the top of the cluster. Twist all the stems tightly. Wind additional wire around the stems, if needed, to secure.
3. Place the stems in the hole in the metal circle on the top of the pot. Adjust stem heights.
4. Remove flowers, squirt glue down the hole, and insert the stems. Add more glue, if needed. Crumple some newspaper and use it to support the leaves and hold them in place until dry. ❑

CAT CROSSING

garden ornament

A delight for any cat lover, this garden ornament makes a great gift.

By Patty Cox

SUPPLIES

1/8" armature wire
28 gauge gold wire
Needlenose pliers
3/4" dowel

INSTRUCTIONS

1. Beginning at coil on cat's back, bend armature wire for cat shape according to pattern. Where wires meet on cat's back, bend wire down at a 90-degree angle. Cut wire end, leaving 1 yd. for the stand.
2. Join wires at top of cat's back with a connecting wrap.
3. Join vertical wire where it crosses the cat's tummy with an x-shaped connecting wrap.
4. Cut two 12" pieces armature wire. Bend each into an s-shape as shown on pattern. Join each s-shape to vertical wire and cat frame with connecting wraps.
5. Wrap stand end of wire around a 3/4" dowel, leaving 3" at the end straight to insert in ground. ❏

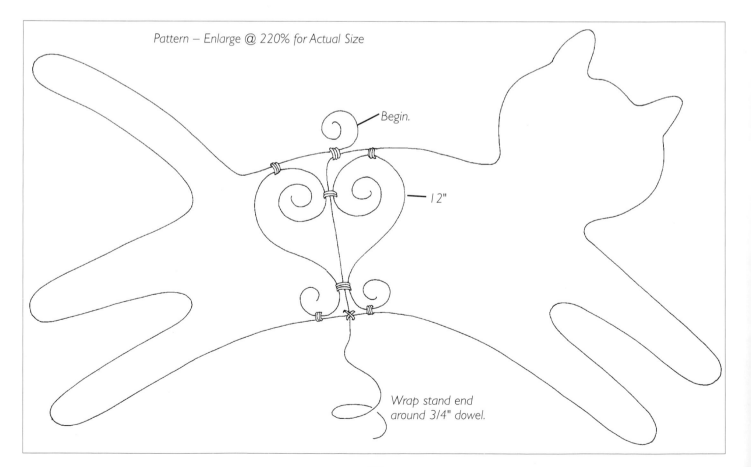

Pattern – Enlarge @ 220% for Actual Size

Begin.

12"

Wrap stand end around 3/4" dowel.

SUNFLOWERS

garden ornaments

These rustic sunflowers look great grouped in a vase or arranged in your garden as art.

By Anne McCloskey

SUPPLIES

Supplies are for one flower:
Paddle of 18 gauge black or rusted wire
20 gauge silver wire
24 gauge silver wire
Wooden disc, 3" diameter, 1/8" think
Metal rod, 1/4" diameter, 16" long
Acrylic craft paint - black, rust
Paint brushes
Brush-on acrylic varnish
Wire cutters
Needlenose pliers

INSTRUCTIONS

Instructions are for one flower. Repeat for as many flowers as you would like to make.

Make Petals:

1. Cut nine 15" pieces of 18 gauge wire for each flower.
2. By hand or with pliers, shape each wire into a figure 8. (This gives you two petals.) (Fig. 1) Secure the center of each figure 8 with 24 gauge wire.
3. Stack 3 figure 8s together, one atop the other, to form a cluster. Make three clusters for each flower (18 petals). Wire together at center.
4. Lay one *cluster* diagonally across another and wire together where they intersect. (Fig. 2) Lay the other cluster atop the others diagonally and wire together to form a basic flower shape. (Fig. 3) Fan out the petals so that flower has a uniform look.

Make Flower Centers:

1. Paint both sides of the wooden disc

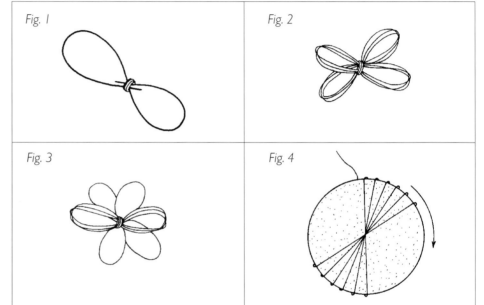

Fig. 1

Fig. 2

Fig. 3

Fig. 4

with black paint. Let dry.

2. Bring the end of a paddle of 20 gauge wire around to the back and hold it securely. In a clockwise direction, slowly pull and wind the wire around the disc. (Not too much – you will want to see the black disc through the wire.) (Fig. 4) When you come back to where you began, twist wire to secure and snip off the end.

Assemble:

1. Apply a large glob of glue to the center of one set of wired petals. Place a disc on top of the glue and press. Place a heavy object on it to hold it in place and let dry.
2. Apply glue along the center of the back of the disc. Press a rod firmly in the glue to make a stem. Be sure the rod does not extend beyond the disc on the top. Let dry.

Paint & Seal:

1. To create the weathered look, dab the rust paint heavily on the discs, lightly stroke paint on the wire on the centers, and dab paint on the petals and stems. Let dry.
2. Turn the flowers over. Dab rust paint on the backs of the petals, stems, and over the glued areas to disguise them. Let dry.
3. Apply varnish all around stem areas to seal them. (You do not need to varnish any other areas.) Let dry. ❏

STAINED GLASS DRAGONFLIES

pin & plant poke

Using pre-cut stained glass shapes, purchased at a craft store, makes this pin and plant poke extra easy to make. If you can't find pre-cut glass shapes, you can cut them yourself or have them cut at a stained glass shop.

By Patty Cox

Dragonfly Pin

SUPPLIES

Pre-cut stained glass dragonfly
24 gauge gold wire
35 dark blue seed beads
Pin back
Jewelry glue
Needlenose pliers

INSTRUCTIONS

1. Wrap wire diagonally around dragonfly body.
2. Wrap wire diagonally around body in the opposite direction, adding seed beads as you wrap. End wire on the underside of body by pulling wire through wraps.
3. Wrap each wing, starting at the end that will be nearest the body. Wrap diagonally to the other end, then double back and wrap diagonally to where you started. Leave a wire tail for securing wings to body.
4. Secure wing wires on center body back. Tighten wires by grasping loose wire wraps with the tip of a needlenose pliers and twisting the pliers.
5. Glue a pin back to back of body. ❑

Dragonfly Plant Poke

SUPPLIES

Pre-cut stained glass dragonfly
22 gauge silver wire
Needlenose pliers

INSTRUCTIONS

1. Cut two 1-1/2 yard lengths silver wire. Make a 90-degree bend in each wire about 1-1/2" from the end. Place bent ends on the underside of dragonfly body back, placing bends at each end of body. (Fig. 1) Wrap wire around each end of dragonfly, meeting wires at center back. Twist wires a few times to secure. Leave wire tails attached.
2. Wrap each wing individually, bending wire over the tip end of each wing and wrapping the wire around the wing toward the body. Leave a wire tail about 12" long.
3. Twist all wire tails together to make the poke. Tighten wires by grasping loose wire wraps with the tip of a needlenose pliers and twisting pliers. ❑

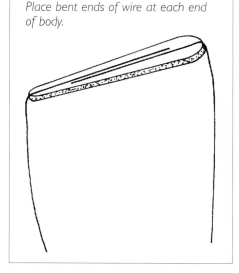

Fig. 1 - Dragonfly back wire placement

Place bent ends of wire at each end of body.

LILY

beaded flower

This dramatic flower – made with seeds beads and wire – won't wilt or fade.

By Diana Thomas

SUPPLIES

Yellow seed beads, 1 oz.
Green seed beads, 3-1/2 oz.
Seed beads, 1/2 oz. of each color -
   gold, orange, and red
32 gauge wire
18 gauge floral wire
Green floral tape
Masking tape
Wire cutters
Flat-nosed pliers

INSTRUCTIONS

Make the Stamen:

1. Thread 3 red beads on the center of a 10" piece of 32 gauge wire. Loop wire back through the beads and twist wires together.
2. Thread 32 red beads on both wires.
3. To finish, thread 1 red bead on only one wire. Bring the two wires together again and twist together to hold in place.
4. Repeat steps 1-3 six more times.
5. Hold all end wires together and twist together, using pliers, to form completed stamen.

Make the Petals:

Each petal is made of seven inside pieces and an edge piece. See Fig. 1 a-e. You will make six petals in all. Repeat these steps for each petal.

1. To make piece A, thread 1 yellow bead on the center of a 12" piece of 32 gauge wire, then loop wire back through the bead and twist wires together.
2. Thread on both wires: 21 gold , 1 red, 5 orange, 1 red, 3 gold, 1 red, 5 orange, 1 red, 3 gold, 1 red, 5 orange, 1 red, 3 gold.
3. To finish, thread 1 yellow bead on only

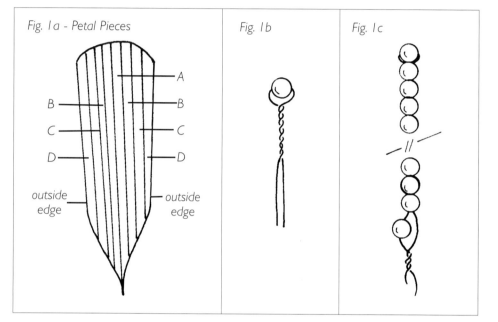

Fig. 1a - Petal Pieces — A, B, C, D — outside edge — outside edge

Fig. 1b

Fig. 1c

one wire. Bring the two wires together and twist to hold in place.

4. To make piece B, thread 1 yellow bead on the center of a 12" piece of 32 gauge wire, then loop wire back through the bead and twist wires together.
5. Thread on both wires: 27 gold, 1 red, 5 orange, 1 red, 3 gold, 1 red, 5 orange, 1 red, 3 gold.
6. To finish, thread 1 yellow bead on only one wire. Bring the two wires together and twist to hold in place,
7. Repeat steps 4-6 to make second B piece.
8. To make piece C, thread 1 yellow bead on the center of a 12" piece of 32 gauge wire, then loop wire back through the bead and twist wires together.
9. Thread on both wires: 5 gold, 1 yellow, 5 gold, 1 yellow, 5 gold, 1 yellow, 5 gold, 1 yellow, 5 gold, 1 yellow, 1 red,

5 orange, 1 red, 3 gold.

10. To finish, thread 1 yellow bead on only one wire. Bring the two wires together and twist to hold in place.
11. To make second C piece, repeat steps 8-10.
12. To make piece D, thread 1 yellow bead on the center of a 12" piece of 32 gauge wire, then loop wire back through the bead and twist wires together.
13. Thread on both wires: 1 gold, 5 yellow, 1 gold, 5 yellow, 1 gold, 5 yellow, 1 gold, 5 yellow, 1 gold, 5 yellow, 1 gold, 5 yellow.
14. To finish, thread 1 yellow bead on only one wire. Bring the two wires together and twist to hold in place.
15. To make second D piece, repeat steps 12-14.

Continued on page 74

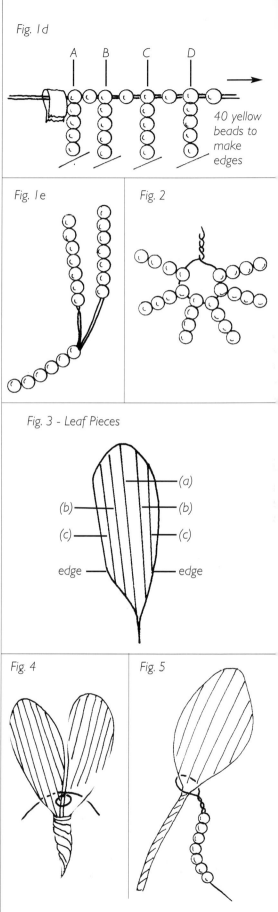

Fig. 1d

A   B   C   D

40 yellow beads to make edges

Fig. 1e

Fig. 2

Fig. 3 - Leaf Pieces

(a)

(b)   (b)

(c)   (c)

edge   edge

Fig. 4

Fig. 5

continued from page 72

Assemble the Petals:

Assemble the petals one at a time, repeating these steps for each petal.

1. Cut a 36" piece of 32 gauge wire and fold in half, using pliers to flatten fold. This will be the outside edge of the petal.
2. Use a small piece of masking tape in the center of the doubled wires to hold beads in place temporarily.
3. Thread on both wires: the top bead of piece A, 1 yellow bead, the top bead of piece B, 1 yellow bead, the top bead of piece C, 1 yellow bead, the top bead of piece D, 40 yellow beads. Hold end wires of D with edge wires and thread 6 yellow beads on all. Hold end wires of C with D and edge wires and thread 6 yellow beads on all. Hold end wires of A, B, C, and D with edge wires and thread 3 yellow beads on all.
4. Hold end wires of A, B, C, and D with edge wires and twist together with pliers to hold.
5. Remove tape from center and starting on other side, repeat step 3 to connect B, C, and D.
6. Hold all end wires and twist together with pliers to hold.

Make the Bud:

1. Thread 1 gold bead on the center of a 12" piece of 32 gauge wire, then loop wire back through the bead.
2. Thread 34 orange beads and 12 green beads on each wire end. Hold end wires and twist with pliers to hold.
3. Repeat steps 1 and 2 five more times.
4. Thread a 4" piece of 32 gauge wire through the gold bead at the top of each piece. Pull tight and twist together to hold. Cut off extra wire. (Fig. 2)
5. Hold all end wires and twist together with pliers to secure.

Make the Leaves:

Each leaf is made of five inside pieces and an edge piece. See Fig. 3. You will make two leaves. Repeat the steps for each leaf.

1. To make piece (a), thread 1 green bead on the center of a 12" piece of 32 gauge wire, then loop wire back through the bead and twist wires together.
2. Thread on both wires: 47 green beads.
3. To finish, thread 1 green bead on only one wire. Bring the two wires together and twist to hold in place.
4. To make (b), thread 1 green bead on the center of a 12" piece of 32 gauge wire, then loop wire back through the bead and twist wires together.
5. Thread on both wires: 39 green beads.
6. To finish, thread 1 green bead on only one wire. Bring the two wires together and twist to hold in place.
7. To make second (b) piece, repeat steps 4-6.
8. To make piece (c): thread 1 green bead on the center of a 12" piece of 32 gauge wire, then loop wire back through the bead and twist wires together.
9. Thread on both wires: 35 green beads.
10. To finish, thread 1 green bead on only one wire. Bring the two wires together and twist to hold in place.

Assemble the Leaves:

Assemble the leaves one at a time, repeating the steps for each leaf.

1. Cut a 24" piece of 32 gauge wire. Fold in half, using pliers to flatten fold. This will be the outside edge of the leaf.
2. Use a small piece of masking tape in the center of the doubled wires to hold beads in place temporarily.
3. Thread on both wires: the top bead of piece (a), 3 green beads, the top bead of piece (b), 3 green beads, the top bead of piece (c), 38 green beads. Wrap end wires of (c) around edge wires twice. Cut off excess. Thread 3 green beads on edge wires. Wrap end wires of (b) around edge wires twice. Cut off excess. Thread 3 green beads on edge wires.
4. Hold end wires of (a), (b), (c) with edge wires and twist together with pliers to hold.
5. Remove tape from center and starting on other side, repeat step 3 to connect (b) and (c).
6. Hold all end wires and twist together with pliers to hold.

Assemble the Flower:

1. Cut an 11" piece of floral wire and use pliers to fold 1/2" over on one end. Wrap end wires of stamen unit around this end of floral wire. Wrap with floral tape to secure.
2. Hold petals in place around stamen. Wrap an 18" piece of 32 gauge wire around end wires. Wrap with floral tape to secure.
3. At 1/4" above tape, secure each petal to the next by looping a 18" piece of 32 gauge wire around the edge wires of each. (Fig. 4)
4. Bring wire across the back of the petal to secure the next two edges, working all the way around. Cut off excess wire.
5. Cut a 4-1/2" piece of floral wire. Use pliers to fold 1/2" over on one end. Wrap end wires of one leaf around this end of floral wire. Wrap with floral tape to secure. Bend floral wire about 1" below leaf.
6. Hold leaf 2" below base of flower, leaving a 2" stem for leaf. Use an 18" piece of 32 gauge wire to wrap around floral wires. Wrap with floral tape to secure.
7. Cut a 10" piece of floral wire and use pliers to fold 1/2" over on one end. Wrap end wires of bud around this end of floral wire. Wrap with floral tape to secure. Bend floral wire about 3" below bud.
8. Cut a 3" piece of floral wire. Use pliers to fold 1/2" over on one end. Wrap end wires of second leaf around this end of floral wire. Wrap with floral tape to secure. Bend floral wire about 1" below leaf.
9. Hold leaf 1-1/2" below base of bud, leaving a 1-1/2" stem for leaf, and use a 18" piece of 32 gauge wire to wrap around floral wires. Wrap with floral tape to secure.
10. Hold bud stem 4-1/2" below base of flower, leaving a 3" stem for the bud. Use an 18" piece of 32 gauge wire to wrap around floral wires. Wrap with floral tape to secure.

Wrap Stem:

The stem is wrapped with 32 gauge wire threaded with green beads.

1. Begin with one leaf. Bring one end of wire around base of leaf and twist together. Thread with beads and wrap tightly to cover to flower stem. Wrap unbeaded end around stem to secure and cut wire. (Fig. 5)
2. On second leaf, bring one end of wire around base of leaf and twist. Thread with beads and wrap tightly to cover to bud stem. Wrap unbeaded end around stem to secure and cut wire.
3. On bud stem, bring one end of wire around base of bud and twist together. Thread with beads and wrap tightly to cover to flower stem. Wrap unbeaded end around stem to secure and cut wire.
4. On flower stem, bring one end of wire around base of flower and twist together. Thread with beads and wrap tightly to cover to flower stem. Wrap unbeaded end around stem end to secure and cut wire. ❑

HANGING HEART

wall sconce

This wall sconce is made with a glass insulator – the kind once commonly used for electrical wires – turned upside down. You could also use an insulator made of porcelain.

By Patty Cox

SUPPLIES

1/8" armature wire, 24"
24 gauge gold wire
Needlenose pliers
Glass insulator

INSTRUCTIONS

See Fig. 1.

1. Bend the center of armature wire length around the groove in the glass insulator, meeting ends at back. Secure wires with a connecting wrap.

2. Bend wire ends up the back of insulator. Secure wires at the top edge of the insulator with a connecting wrap. Add a small loop for hanging with 24 gauge wire.

3. Bend the ending wires inward, creating two sides of a heart. Secure heart wires at center with a connecting wrap. ❏

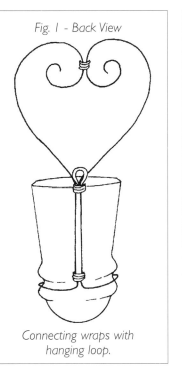

Fig. 1 - Back View

Connecting wraps with hanging loop.

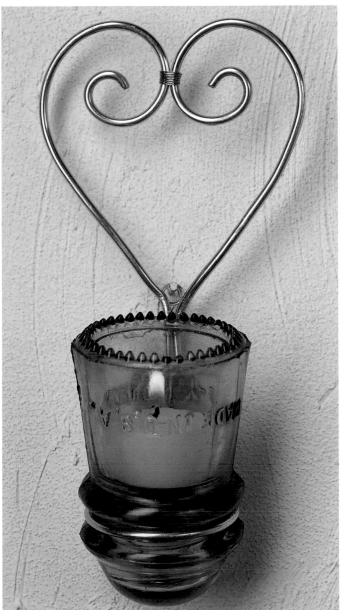

GARDEN LIGHTS

candle holders

Votives will stay lit even when there's a breeze. Make several of these to light up your garden on summer evenings.

By Vivian Peritts

SUPPLIES

For each hanging votive:
3 yds. 18 gauge copper wire
3 yds. 14 gauge aluminum wire
1 yds. 28 gauge tinned copper wire
5 beads - assorted colors and sizes
1 "donut" bead, 3/4" diameter
1 clear glass flowerpot-shaped votive
    holder, 2-1/2" x 2-1/2"
Needlenose pliers
Wire cutters

INSTRUCTIONS

1. Cut three 1 yd. pieces 14 gauge wire.
2. Make a finger loop at the center of one wire piece and twist the wire twice. (Fig. 1) Add the donut-shaped bead.
3. Arrange the centers of all three 14-gauge wires across the bottom of the votive holder. Spread the six wires evenly around the sides of the votive holder. Bring all ends together at the top.
4. Interlock wires around the rim of the votive holder. See Fig. 2.
5. Gather the ends of the wires together. Bend wires to form curves. See Fig. 3.
6. Fold one piece of wire to make a loop 2" long. Wrap another wire around the rest. Fold down the remaining wires and cut them off 1/2" below the fold.
7. Wrap 3 yds. of copper wire around the wire ends below the top loop for about 2".
8. Use 28 gauge wire to attach the beads

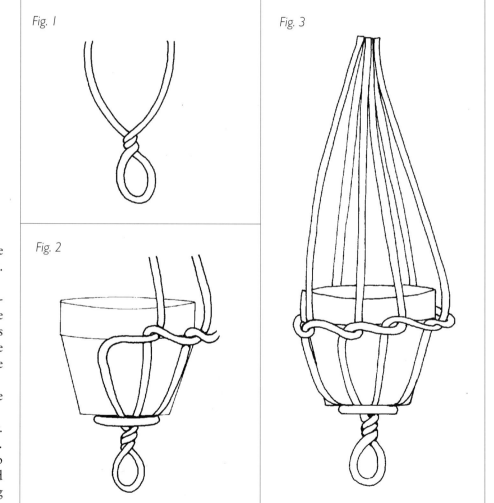

Fig. 1

Fig. 2

Fig. 3

to the interlocking wires around the glass votive holder.
9. Position the votive and arrange the wires. *Tip:* To make a chain of votive holders, connect them with metal S-hooks. ❑

WIRE & STONES

picture frame

Use wire and polished stones to create a rustic frame that's just right for displaying pressed dried flowers, fern fronds, or leaves to create a seasonal display. It can also display a photo.

By Vivian Peritts

SUPPLIES

10-1/2 ft. 14 gauge aluminum-colored wire
4-1/2 yds. 20 gauge aluminum-colored wire
3 polished stones, 1"
1 polished stone, 2"
Rough-surface plywood or barn board, 3/4" thick, 9-1/2" x 13"
Glass, 8" x 10"
8 wood screws, #6 x 5/8"
8 washers, #6
Acrylic paint - off white
Paint brush
Jewelry glue
Needlenose pliers
Dried leaves, flowers, or fern fronds
Colored paper, 7-1/4" x 9-1/4"

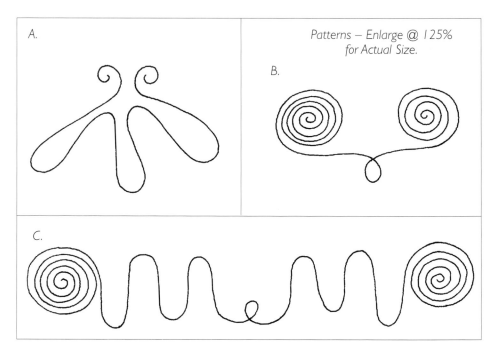

A.

B.

Patterns – Enlarge @ 125% for Actual Size.

C.

INSTRUCTIONS

Cut & Form Wire:

1. Cut 14 gauge wire into one piece 45" long (pattern C), two pieces 24" long (pattern B), and two pieces 14" long (pattern A).
2. Form pieces according to patterns. Press back center loop of A pieces so the loop bends back over itself and creates a holder for a stone.
3. Cut two 1 yd. pieces of 20 gauge wire. Curl one end of one piece into a tight coil. Place the coil on top of a 1" stone. Place stone on the folded loop of one piece A. Wrap the remaining wire around the stone and the 14 gauge wire piece. Repeat with second piece of 36" wire, a 1" stone, and the remaining piece A. Set aside.
4. Cut a 1 yd. piece of 20 gauge wire. Tightly coil both ends. Place one coil on top of a 1" stone. Place the stone between the coils of one of the B pieces. Use the wire to secure the stone in place, ending up with the second coiled end on top of the stone. Set aside.
5. Coil both ends of the remaining 1-1/2 yds. of 20 gauge wire. Place one coil on top of the 2" stone. Place the stone at the center of the A piece. Use the wire to secure the stone in place, ending up with the second coiled end on top of the stone.
6. Use glue to secure the bottoms of the stones to the wire pieces that hold them. Let dry.

Paint Wood:

Thin acrylic paint with water to make a stain. Brush thinned paint over front and edges of wood. Let dry.

Assemble:

1. Arrange paper, dried materials, and glass on wood, using photo as a guide.
2. Arrange wire pieces on wood, overlapping glass as shown in photo. Attach with screws, placing a washer between the wire and each screw. ❑

Kitchen & Bath

Wire and beads can add color and shine to your table and bathroom. In this section, you'll see a gorgeous collection of seashell-trimmed wire bath accessories, table decorations, and imaginative ways to embellish food gifts.

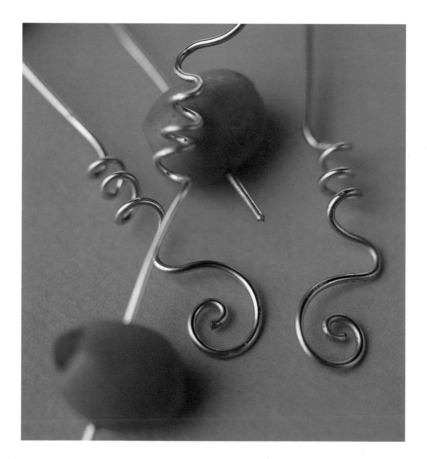

Pictured at right: Beach Shells Bathroom Accessories. See pages 82 & 84 for instructions. Additional photos on pages 83 and 84.

BEACH SHELLS

bathroom accessories

This functional and decorative set for the bathroom includes a soap dish, a hand towel tray, a candle holder, and decorative bottles. Hammering the armature wire not only makes the pieces stronger, but imparts an attractive forged look. The aluminum wire and mesh are pliable, easy to form, and rustproof.

By Marie Browning

GENERAL SUPPLIES

(for the Set)
1/4" diamond-pattern aluminum wire
    mesh
3/16" armature wire
20 gauge silver-colored wire
24 gauge silver-colored wire
Wire cutters
Roundnose pliers
Ruler
Hammer
Jewelry glue or other strong
    silicone-based glue

Shell Soap Dish

SUPPLIES

Large clam shell, 5" diameter
7-10 small shells
Plus General Supplies listed for the set

INSTRUCTIONS

1. Cut two 20" pieces 3/16" armature wire. Cut one 12" piece 20 gauge wire.
2. Using the pattern provided, form the armature wire pieces.
3. With a hammer, flatten all the coils.
4. Hold these two pieces at 90-degrees to each other, and to the surface so that they cross in the center and form an X. Notice where they cross. Separate the two pieces and still holding them at a 90-degree angle to surface, hammer the pieces flat where they cross.
5. Cross the wire pieces in the middle. With the 20 gauge wire, wrap at the center where they cross to secure and form the holder.
6. Glue the smaller shells on the large bowl-shaped clam shell to decorate.
7. Place the large shell in the wire holder, adjusting the wire to fit. ❏

Wire Mesh Bottles

SUPPLIES

For each bottle:
Bottle with cork top
Shells to decorate cork
Plus General Supplies listed for the set

INSTRUCTIONS

1. Cut a piece of wire mesh large enough to fit around the circumference of the bottle with 1" extra at the top and bottom. Cut a piece of armature wire long enough to fit neck of bottle plus 6" for the coil.
2. Form a coil at the end of the armature wire, using the pattern provided. Hammer the coil flat, leaving the remaining wire to wrap around the neck of the bottle. Set aside.
3. Wrap the mesh around the bottle and form tightly to shape. Trim away excess.
4. With the 24 gauge wire, "sew" the mesh, weaving in and out to join the two ends securely.
5. Wrap the wire piece around the neck of the bottle and arrange the coil in the front.
6. Glue shells on the cork to decorate. *Option:* Glue a tiny shell on the end of the coil. ❏

Additional project instructions follow on page 84.

Wire Mesh Bottle & Scoop

Wire Mesh Bottle & Bubble Blower

Hand Towel Tray & Shell Soap Dish

Seascape Candle Holder

SUPPLIES

Glass cylinder vase, 4" high, 4" diameter
Glass tea light holder
Tea light candle
White sand
Selection of small shells and sea glass pieces
Plus General Supplies listed for the set

INSTRUCTIONS

1. Cut a 6" square piece of aluminum mesh. Cut two 7" pieces of armature wire. Cut a 12" piece of 20 gauge silver wire.
2. Hammer flat the two pieces of armature wire.
3. Using the pattern provided, form the wire pieces.
4. Form the mesh to fit snugly inside the glass cylinder vase. Trim away excess mesh above the rim.
5. Cross the wire pieces in the middle. With 20 gauge wire, wrap them where they intersect to secure and form the holder. Place the formed mesh on the wire holder. Secure with wire.
6. Pour the sand in the vase. Arrange the shells to create your seascape.
7. Place the wire and mesh holder in the vase. Adjust as needed to fit.

8. Place the candle in the glass holder. Place candle holder on the wire and mesh holder. ❑

Bubble Blower

SUPPLIES

Glass beads and small shells
Plus General Supplies listed for the set

INSTRUCTIONS

1. Cut a 5" piece of armature wire.
2. Using pattern provided, coil wire to form handle.
3. Flatten the piece with a hammer.
4. Form a circle with a 20 gauge piece of wire.
5. Secure circle to the coiled handle with 24 gauge wire. Continue to coil the 24 gauge wire down the handle, adding glass beads and small shells to accent. ❑

Shell Scoop for Bath Salts

SUPPLIES

1 small clamshell
1 smaller shell
Plus General Supplies listed for the set

INSTRUCTIONS

1. Cut a 5" piece of armature wire.
2. Coil wire to form a handle.
3. Flatten the piece with a hammer. Hammer the uncoiled end very flat to form a surface to adhere the shell.
4. Glue clamshell to the handle. Glue the small shell to the clamshell as shown in photo to strengthen and embellish your scoop. ❑

Hand Towel Tray

SUPPLIES

2 shells, 2" long
Plus General Supplies listed for the set

INSTRUCTIONS

1. Cut armature wire into these pieces:
   Base - one 24" piece, one 7" piece.
   Decorative sides - two 20" pieces, two 14" pieces.
   Cut a piece of wire mesh 9" x 7".
2. Using the patterns provided, form the small and large side pieces.
3. With a hammer, flatten all the coils. Holding the pieces at a 90-degree angle to the surface, hammer flat the parts of the pieces that will fit together along the bottom of each piece.

Continued on next page

BEACH SHELLS

Patterns – Actual Size

Shell Soap Dish

Sides of Hand Towel Tray

Candle Holder

*Sides of
Hand Towel Tray*

*Coil for Bottles,
Scoop, and
Bubble Blower*

Hand Towel Tray (cont.)

4. Bend the smaller piece at the center to a point. Attach the smaller (inner) side piece to the larger side piece by wrapping with 20 gauge wire. Wrap at bottom where they touch and wrap at sides of coils. (Fig. 1) Set aside.

5. Form the 24" base wire piece into a 5" x 7" rectangle. Hammer flat. (Fig. 2)

6. Flatten the 7" base piece and fold up each end 1". Fig. 3.

7. Position one decorative side piece on the base. Secure with 20 gauge wire. Repeat with remaining side piece.

8. Place the connected base and sides on the mesh piece. Fold the mesh up around the bottom to make a tray.

9. Attach the 7" base piece under the middle of the tray. (This piece strengthens the construction and provides the armatures the decorative shells are attached to.)

10. Use 24 gauge wire to "sew" the 7" base piece to the underside of the tray.

11. Glue a shell to each of the turned-up ends of the 7" base piece. ❑

Fig. I wrap

wrap

Fig. 2

Fig. 3

WIRED FOR ENTERTAINING

napkin ring and cocktail skewers

Here are two ways wire can be used to dress up a buffet table. When making sets of napkin rings, you can use stones of one color or many. How pretty your appetizers will look skewered with these wonderful picks.

By Patty Cox

Cocktail Skewers

SUPPLIES

For each:
16 gauge buss wire, 6" long
Roundnose pliers

INSTRUCTIONS

1. Hold end of 6" wire length with roundnose pliers. Coil end of wire according to pattern.
2. Wrap wire vertically three times around roundnose pliers, leaving other end of wire straight. Remove wire from pliers and shape as needed. ❑

Pattern – Actual Size

Napkin Ring

SUPPLIES

For each ring:
Translucent glass stone
20" 16 gauge buss wire
24 gauge gold wire
Needlenose pliers
Jewelry glue
2 cotter pins, 2" x 3/16"
1 fender washer, 11/4" x 3/16"

INSTRUCTIONS

1. Cut two 24" pieces buss wire. Form each end of one piece into leaves, according to pattern. Form one end of the other wire into a leaf.
2. Secure leaves at their stem ends by wrapping with 24 gauge wire. (Fig. 1)
3. Hold the two wires together with leaves together. Twist the wires together, holding wires securely in cotter pins. (Fig. 2) Form this into a ring.
4. Wrap 24 gauge gold wire around a translucent stone. Tighten wire by grasping the wire wrap at the back with needlenose pliers, then twist at a 90º angle.
5. Attach wire to napkin ring.
6. Secure stone with glue.

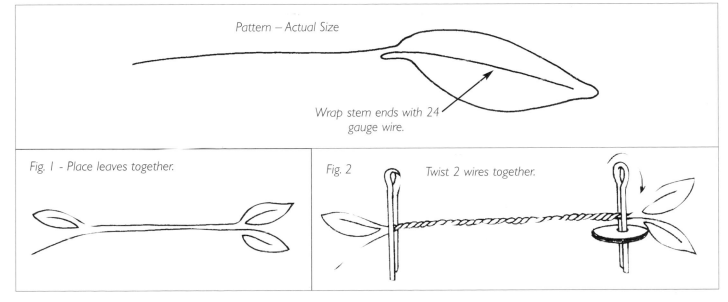

Pattern – Actual Size

Wrap stem ends with 24 gauge wire.

Fig. 1 - Place leaves together.

Fig. 2   Twist 2 wires together.

GIFTS FROM THE KITCHEN

decorated bottles & jars

It's easy to use wire and beads to decorate bottles and jars. Whether they hold homemade or purchased gourmet goodies, these decorated bottles and jars make attractive presents. And gift wrap is unnecessary!

By Vivian Peritts

Wine or Olive Oil Bottle

SUPPLIES

14 gauge copper wire, 45"
20 gauge copper wire, 30"
20 large-hole glass beads - assorted colors and sizes
Amber silver-lined rocaille beads with large holes
Wine bottle or olive oil bottle
Jewelry glue

INSTRUCTIONS

1. Wrap 14 gauge wire around the neck of the bottle as shown in the photo.
2. Glue two beads on the bottom end of the wire.
3. Load the center area of the 20 gauge wire with enough beads to go around the top of the bottle, alternating glass beads with amber beads. Twist ends of the wire together four or five times.
4. Wrap one end around the bottle several times, ending on the opposite side of the bottle from where you started.
5. Thread alternating beads on the other end of the wire, using enough beads to go over the top of the bottle. Twist the two ends of the wire together several times. Cut off one end.
6. Twist the remaining wire end several more times to cover the cut wire and to secure the beads over the lid. Cut off the excess and tuck in the end of the wire. ❑

Condiment Jar

SUPPLIES

14 gauge brown wire, 36"
18 gauge brown wire, 36"
Large hole glass beads assorted sizes and colors
Amber silver-lined rocaille beads with large holes
Pint jar
Needlenose pliers

INSTRUCTIONS

1. Use the pliers to bend the 14 gauge wire into the wavy design of the pattern. Place wire around the jar and interlock ends.
2. Thread the beads on the center area of the 18 gauge wire, alternating amber beads and glass beads. Weave the beaded wire in and out of the wave design. Twist ends together where they meet around the jar neck. Cut off one end.
3. Thread beads, alternating amber and glass beads, on the remaining end.
4. Stretch across the top of the jar and secure on the other side. Trim off the excess wire. ❑

Condiment Bottle

You can use the same supplies to decorate a bottle that contains catsup, mustard, or a salad dressing. Follow the instructions for the tall bottle, using 96" of 14 gauge wire. ❑

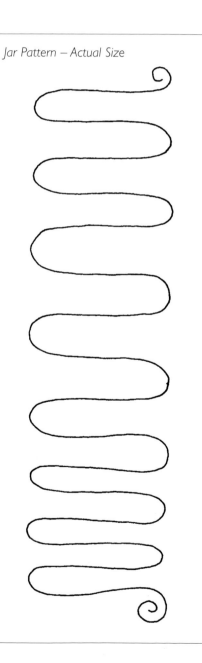

Jar Pattern – Actual Size

BEADS & LACE

pitcher & glass covers

The weight of the beads holds these vintage-inspired covers in place. Use them to keep flying insects out of drinks when you're serving outdoors. The number of beads and the amount of wire or thread you need will vary, depending on the size of the doily. Choose beads to coordinate with your tableware.

By Damema Spragens

Pitcher

SUPPLIES

For each:
200 blue assorted seed beads, size 11
12 assorted blue glass beads, 6mm-8mm
1 silver crimping bead
1 crocheted doily, 6" diameter
40" beading wire, .010 diameter
Beading needle
Wire cutters
Tape measure

INSTRUCTIONS

1. Measure and mark 12 equally spaced spots along the outside of the doily. They are where the beads will hang.
2. Fold wire in half. String on a seed bead to mark the halfway point.
3. String a glass bead on both wires. Pull down to seed bead.
4. String 5 seed beads on both wires. Pull down to glass bead.
5. String 5 seed beads on each wire, creating a V-shape. (Fig. 1)
6. Hang the V from the edge of the doily, pulling it tight by weaving the left and right wires along the edge of the lace. Weave the right wire to the spot you've marked for the next bead to hang.
7. Place the beading needle on the wire and string on 10 seed beads, a glass bead, and a seed bead.
8. Sew the wire back through the glass bead and 5 seed beads. String on 5

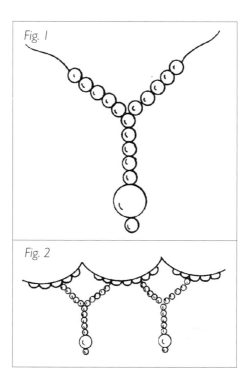

Fig. 1

Fig. 2

seed beads and weave the wire back into the lace edge, pulling the V tight against the lace. (Fig. 2)
9. Continue pattern around the doily until you are 1" from the end of the right wire. Weave the wire along the edge of the doily to conceal.
10. Place needle on left wire and work around from the other side, using the same technique.
11. Place a silver crimp bead on the right wire and string the left wire through the crimp bead. Pull wires tight, being sure to let the lace hang. Crimp bead. Clip off excess wire. ❏

Pitcher Cover

SUPPLIES

Assorted seed beads
Assorted bugle beads
21 larger assorted beads, 6mm-10mm
Crocheted doily, 10" diameter
White thread and beading needle
Scissors

INSTRUCTIONS

Use the shape of the doily to determine the positions of the beads – on this doily, for instance, the beaded trim was placed between the scallops on the lacy edge.

1. Thread needle with double thread and knot end. Take a stitch through the edge of the doily.
2. Thread on 1 bugle bead, 4 seed beads, 1 larger bead, and 1 seed bead. Pass thread back through the larger bead and the 4 seed beads. Add a second bugle bead.
3. Stitch through edge of doily to secure and along edge of doily about 1/4".
4. Thread on 3 bugle beads, 8 seed beads, 1 larger bead, and 1 seed bead. Pass thread back through the larger bead and 4 of the seed beads. Add 4 seed beads and 3 bugle beads.
5. Stitch through edge of doily to secure and along edge of doily about 1/4".
6. Repeat step #2 to complete one section of the trim. Knot thread and cut.
7. Move on to the next area where you plan to place beads and repeat steps 1-6.
8. Repeat to complete doily. ❏

Around the House

The versatility of wire and beads is evident in the projects in this section. There are wonderful lampshades, both vintage-inspired and contemporary, plus candle holders and candlesticks and wire-scroll accessories for wall and tabletop.

Pictured at right: Terra Cotta Timepiece Clock and Recycled Ashtray Candle Holder. See pages 94 and 95 for instructions.

TERRA COTTA TIMEPIECE

clock

Pictured on page 93

This project uses a terra cotta saucer and a battery-powered clock mechanism to create a bejeweled clock.

By Patty Cox

SUPPLIES

1/8" armature wire
24 gauge gold wire
10" terra cotta plant saucer
4 flatbacked frosted green glass marbles, 3/4"
Clock movement, quartz battery powered
Acrylic craft paint - metallic pewter, pale aqua, burnt umber
Paint brushes
Sandpaper
Metallic rub-on wax - antique gold
Drill and 5/16" drill bit
Epoxy glue
Needlenose pliers
Option: Double-sided foam tape and piece of foam core

INSTRUCTIONS

Prepare Saucer:

1. Drill a 5/16" hole in the center of terra cotta saucer.
2. Paint bottom of saucer (which will be the front of the clock) with pewter and pale aqua paints. Let dry.
3. Sand saucer lightly, lifting some of the chalk paint.

Make Wire Squiggles:

1. Wrap flatbacked marbles with 24 gauge gold wire. Tighten wraps by grasping ends of wrapped wire with needlenose pliers and twisting at a 90-degree angle.
2. Bend four pieces armature wire into squiggles according to pattern provided.
3. Dab wire squiggles with burnt umber paint, allowing some of the silver wire to show through. Let dry.
4. Rub antique gold metallic wax over areas of wire squiggles. Let dry.

Assemble:

1. Install clock movement and assemble according to package instructions. *Option:* To make the clock hands sit flush on the terra cotta face, add spacers between the battery pack and the clock face, using layers of foam core and foam tape.
2. Glue wire squiggles on four sides of clock face, aligning the top squiggle with top back of clockworks.
3. Glue wrapped marbles in each wire squiggle as shown. ❏

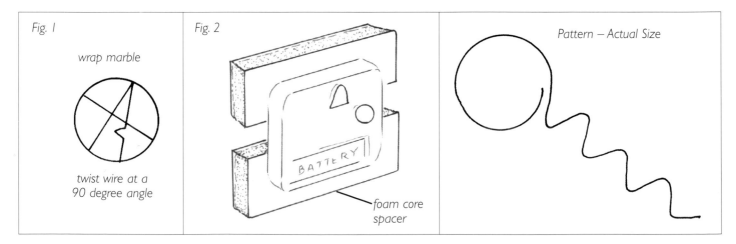

Fig. 1

wrap marble

twist wire at a 90 degree angle

Fig. 2

BATTERY

foam core spacer

Pattern – Actual Size

RECYCLED ASHTRAY

candle holder

Pictured on page 93

Here's a great way to recycle a ceramic ashtray – the wire disguises the original use of the piece and the depressions in the rim that once held cigarettes serve to keep the wire in place.

By Patty Cox

SUPPLIES

1/4" armature wire
24 gauge wire
Paint kit for creating a rusted metal finish
Matte acrylic sealer spray
4" ashtray with 3 depressions in rim
Needlenose pliers
Epoxy glue
Candle

INSTRUCTIONS

1. Cut three 18" lengths armature wire. Bend each into an s-shape according to pattern.
2. Secure the s-shapes together with connecting wraps to make the wire tripod. *Option:* For added stability, add epoxy glue to the inside of wraps. Let dry.
3. Paint wire tripod with rusted metal paint kit, following manufacturer's instructions. Let dry.
4. Spray with matte sealer.
5. Position ashtray in center of tripod. Bend the tops of the s-shapes to fit each depression on ashtray rim.
6. Place candle in ashtray. ❑

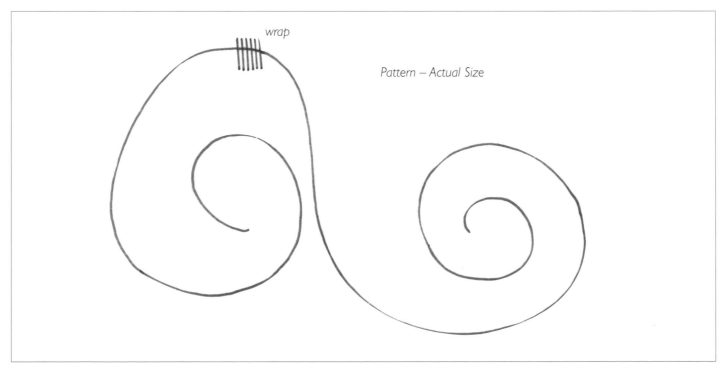

wrap

Pattern – Actual Size

HEART & SCROLLWORK

rack with hooks

A purchased picture frame is used as the base for this rack with three hooks. This one is made so that what is usually the back of the frame is the front.

By Patty Cox

SUPPLIES

1/8" armature wire
24 gauge gold wire
Wooden frame with 4" x 10" opening
  (the size for panoramic photos)
3 coat hooks
6 small screw eyes
Sawtooth hangers
Hammer
Needlenose pliers
Optional: Fine sandpaper

INSTRUCTIONS

1. Cut two 19" pieces armature wire. Bend each into a large s-shape according to pattern.
2. Cut two 12" pieces armature wire. Bend each into a small s-shape according to pattern.
3. Cut one 11" piece armature wire. Bend wire in half. Pound the fold into a point using a hammer. Bend the ends into a heart shape according to pattern.
4. *Option:* Lightly sand armature wire to give it a satin shine.
5. Secure s-shapes and heart together with 24 gauge gold wire, using pattern as a guide.
6. Remove glass and backing from frame. Place wire design in frame. Mark placement for six screw eyes. Remove wire design.

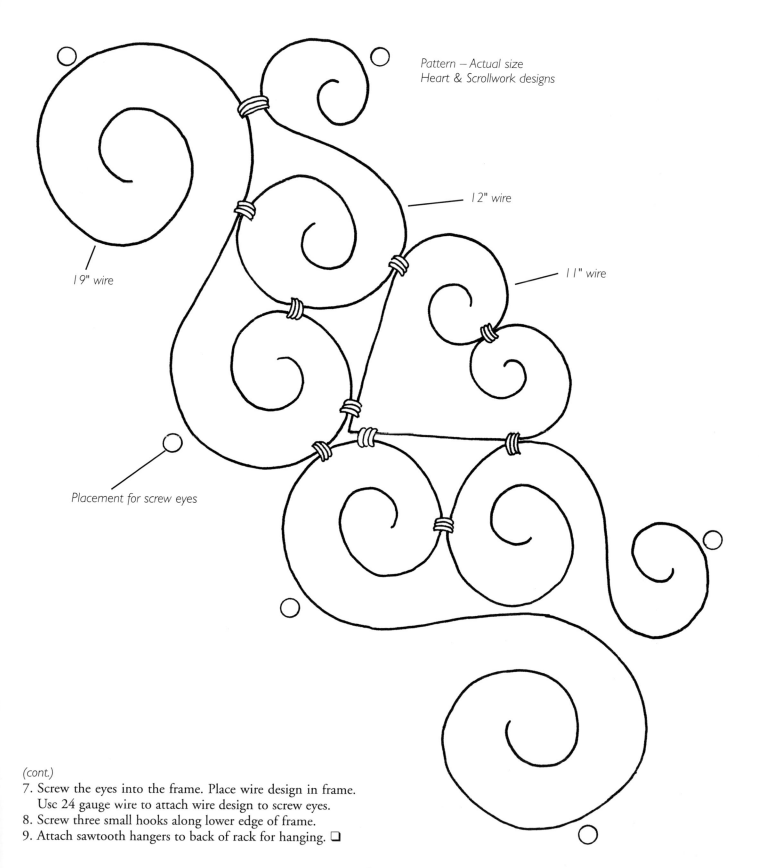

Pattern – Actual size
Heart & Scrollwork designs

12" wire

11" wire

19" wire

Placement for screw eyes

(cont.)
7. Screw the eyes into the frame. Place wire design in frame.
   Usc 24 gauge wire to attach wire design to screw eyes.
8. Screw three small hooks along lower edge of frame.
9. Attach sawtooth hangers to back of rack for hanging. ❑

RED & WIRED

lampshade

Here's a dramatic, contemporary take on the beaded lampshade. It's made with a wire hanging basket usually used for plants. You can find these baskets in garden centers and hardware stores. The addition of a modern metal lampbase adds just the right touch for a contemporary look.

By Vivian Peritts

SUPPLIES

6 yds. red 14 gauge wire
30 yds. red 18 gauge wire
6 iridescent marbles, 1"
18 iridescent marbles, 1/2"
12 iridescent glass buttons, 2"
Black wire hanging basket, 12" diameter
Lamp base with harp
Jewelry glue
Needlenose pliers

INSTRUCTIONS

1. Remove hanging chains from basket. Use for another purpose or recycle.
2. Cut the 14 gauge wire into pieces 1 yd. long. Coil one end of each piece. Coil the other end around a 1" marble. (Fig. 1)
3. Intertwine the 14 gauge wires around the basket. (Fig. 2)
4. Cut the 18 gauge wire into 1 yd. pieces. Coil the ends of 10 of the pieces. Coil the other end of those pieces around a 1/2" marble.
5. Wind each wire between two basket ribs, starting at the bottom on one side and working across the top and down the other side. (Fig. 3) Where the wires criss-cross the top, there should be space for the finial screw of the harp.
6. Locate the center of each of the remaining pieces of 18 gauge wire. Glue a 2" button at the center of each. Let dry.
7. Wrap the wire around each button to secure and coil the ends.
8. Weave the wires through the basket ribs, distributing the wires and buttons evenly around the frame.
9. Weave remaining pieces of 18 gauge wire over the basket frame. Coil the ends.
10. Place shade on lamp base. Attach finial screw. ❏

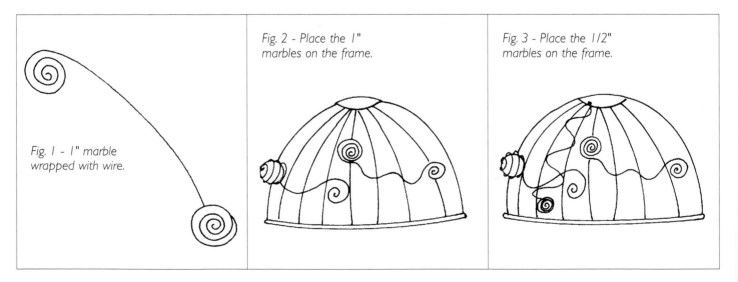

Fig. 1 - 1" marble wrapped with wire.

Fig. 2 - Place the 1" marbles on the frame.

Fig. 3 - Place the 1/2" marbles on the frame.

MARDI GRAS

candle holders

These colorful candlesticks are a centerpiece in themselves. Make them from turned wooden pieces that you glue together or use the technique to decorate a pair of purchased candlesticks.

By Anne McCloskey

SUPPLIES

Either:
2 turned wooden candlesticks, 10" tall
Masking tape
Or:
Turned wooden pieces (top to bottom as shown)
    2 tulip candlecups, 1-15/16" tall
    2 cubes, 1-1/4" tall
    2 flat knobs, 1-3/4" tall
    2 candlecups, 1-5/8" tall
    2 goblet-shape candlecups, 2" tall
    2 flat toy wheels, 2" diameter
    2 nut cups, 2-1/2" diameter
And:
20 gauge gold beading wire
150 assorted iridescent, gold, and pewter beads - various shapes and sizes
4 gold heart charms
30 gold leaf charms
Acrylic craft paints - Fuchsia, lilac, pink, light blue, lavender, gold
Paint brush
Sponge
Palette or disposable foam plate
Gloss varnish
Adhesive suitable for wood and metal
Aluminum foil

INSTRUCTIONS

Paint the Candlesticks:

If you are using turned wood pieces, paint them before assembling. If you're using turned wooden candlesticks, use masking tape to mask off areas as needed.

1. Paint the sections of the candlesticks or turned wooden pieces various colors, using photo as a guide. Let dry.
2. Squeeze out paint colors on palette or foam plate. With a dampened sponge, lightly sponge on contrasting colors, using photo as a guide. Add a little gold to most areas to unify. Let dry.
3. Apply varnish to seal. Let dry.
4. *If you are using turned pieces,* glue them together beginning with the upside-down nut cups at the bottom. See Supplies list for order. Be sure each piece is centered on the one below it. Let glue dry.

Wire the Beads:

1. Cut a piece of wire 3 ft. long. Twist a small loop with a 2" tail in one end.
2. String beads and charms on the wire, using photo as a guide.
3. Glue the wire tail inside the top cup with the first bead sitting at the top of the cup. Crumple a piece of foil into a ball and press it in the cup to hold the wire in place. Let the glue dry.
4. Wind the wire with the beads around the candlestick. Wind the end of the wire near the bottom of the candlestick. Tuck in end and secure with glue.
5. Cut two more 3 ft. pieces of wire. Secure in candle cup at top with glue. Let dry. Wind wires around the candlestick, wind many times around the bottom, tuck in ends, and secure with glue.
6. Repeat the steps to complete the second candlestick. ❏

WORDS TO LIVE BY

hanging ornament

The intricate scroll design frames a suspended disk. The photo shows a round gold-tone disk with an engraved monogram that was purchased at an engraving store. You could, instead, make an ornament with a saying of your choice. Examples are included.

By Patty Cox

SUPPLIES

1/8" armature wire
28 gauge gold wire
2-3/4" gold ring
2-1/2" engraved medallion **or** clear
   plastic button, silver paper, and T-pin
Needlenose pliers

INSTRUCTIONS

1. Cut eight 8" pieces armature wire. Form six s-shapes and two c-shapes according to pattern.
2. Connect scrolls by wrapping with 28 gauge wire as shown.
3. Connect all scrolls around the center 2-3/4" ring by wrapping as shown with 28 gauge wire.
4. Form a small loop for hanging at top back with 28 gauge wire.
5. Hang medallion in the center circle. *Option:* Photocopy the designs from this book onto silver paper or typeset and print on silver paper. (See examples.) Cut silver circle from paper. Place between front and back of clear plastic disk and press button sections together. Push a t-pin through the top center of disk to create a hole. Insert 28 gauge wire through hole. Hang disk in the center of ring.
6. Suspend ornament on a stand or hang on the wall. ❑

Scroll Patterns – Actual Size

Scroll Patterns – Actual Size

*Photo copy these on silver paper, cut out and place between two clear
plastic disks to make a hanging ornament.*

*Love
and
Laughter*

*Faith,
Hope, Love abide.
The greatest of these
is Love.*

*Welcome
to our
Home*

Tropical Colors
Beaded Boxes
Instructions on page 106

TROPICAL COLORS

beaded boxes

Use these wire-framed beaded boxes pictured on page 105 for colorful storage. The short box is 3-1/2" x 4-1/2" x 1-1/2" (perfect for notepaper); the tall box is 3-1/2" square and 4-1/2" tall (great for pens and pencils).

By Pat McMahon

Short Box

SUPPLIES

32 gauge beading wire
16 gauge galvanized wire
6 oz. #8 pale green opaque glass seed beads
3 oz. size #8 turquoise opaque glass seed beads
2 pairs needlenose pliers
Roundnose pliers
Wire cutters
Jewelry glue
Marking pen

To make the wooden jig:
A piece of wood, 6" x 8", 1" thick.
1-1/2" box nails
Ruler
Pencil
Hammer

INSTRUCTIONS

Make the Wooden Jig:

1. Using the ruler, draw a rectangle 4-1/2" x 3-1/2" near one corner of the piece of wood. Pound 1 nail into each corner of the rectangle exactly where the lines cross, using 4 nails in all.
2. Draw a second rectangle 3-1/2" x 1-1/2", leaving plenty of space between the rectangles, and pound nails in each corner as before.
3. Repeat this process for a 4-1/2 " x 1-1/2" rectangle. See Fig. 1.

Form Wire:

1. Cut 2 pieces of 16 gauge wire 13" long. Use the needlenose pliers to fold one of the pieces over at a right angle 2" from

one end. Place this fold against one of the nails of the 3-1/2" x 1-1/2" rectangle on the wooden jig. Fold the wire around the other nails to form a wire rectangle. *Note:* Best results are achieved by using one pair of pliers to hold the wire against the nail and a second pair to bend the wire. See Fig. 2.

2. Holding the wires firmly together at the cut ends, use the marker to mark where the wires overlap. Remove wire from jig. Put a small amount of jewelry glue on the overlap. Press the 2 wires together until the marks are aligned and wrap with a piece of 32 gauge wire. See Fig. 3.
3. Repeat step 2, using the second 13" piece of wire. These are the frames for the narrow sides of the box.
4. Cut 2 pieces of 16 gauge wire 14-1/2" long. Using the same procedure described above, form two wire rectangles with the 4-1/2" x 1-1/2" jig. These are the frames for the long sides of the box.
5. Cut 2 pieces of 16 gauge wire 19-1/2" long. Make 2 more wire rectangles using the 4-1/2" x 3-1/2" jig. These are the top and bottom frames of the box.
6. Cut 1 piece of 16 gauge wire 10" long. Form this piece into a U-shape, using the 4-1/2" x 1-1/2" jig with the 4-1/2" side as the bottom of the U. See Fig. 4. This is the lengthwise side and bottom support.
7. Cut 1 piece of 16 gauge wire 9" long. Make a wire U-shape, using the 3-1/2" x 1-1/2" jig with the 3-1/2" side as the bottom. This is the crosswise support.

Assemble the Frame:

1. Assemble the box frame by joining the sides to the bottom. (Fig. 5.) This is done by wrapping the wires together with 32 gauge wire. (Fig. 6) Use a small amount of glue to secure the ends of the thin wires. Complete the frame by joining the sides to the top the same way.
2. Attach the supports by first marking the center of each side with a marker. Place the small U-shape over the bottom of the box at the center of the longer side. See Fig. 7. Put a small amount of jewelry glue where the support touches each side of the bottom frame. Wrap these joints with 32 gauge wire.
3. Fold the top of the U over at a right angle at the top of the box frame. Position the top of the support at the center mark and, using roundnose pliers, wrap the wire in a loop around the frame. (Fig. 8) Trim excess wire from the loop with wire cutters. Use the flat part of the needlenose pliers to tighten the loop on the frame.
4. Repeat step 3 on the other side of the box.
5. Following the same method, attach the other U-shaped support to the other sides. Wrap the supports where they intersect under the box with 32 gauge wire. (Fig. 9)

Continued on page 108

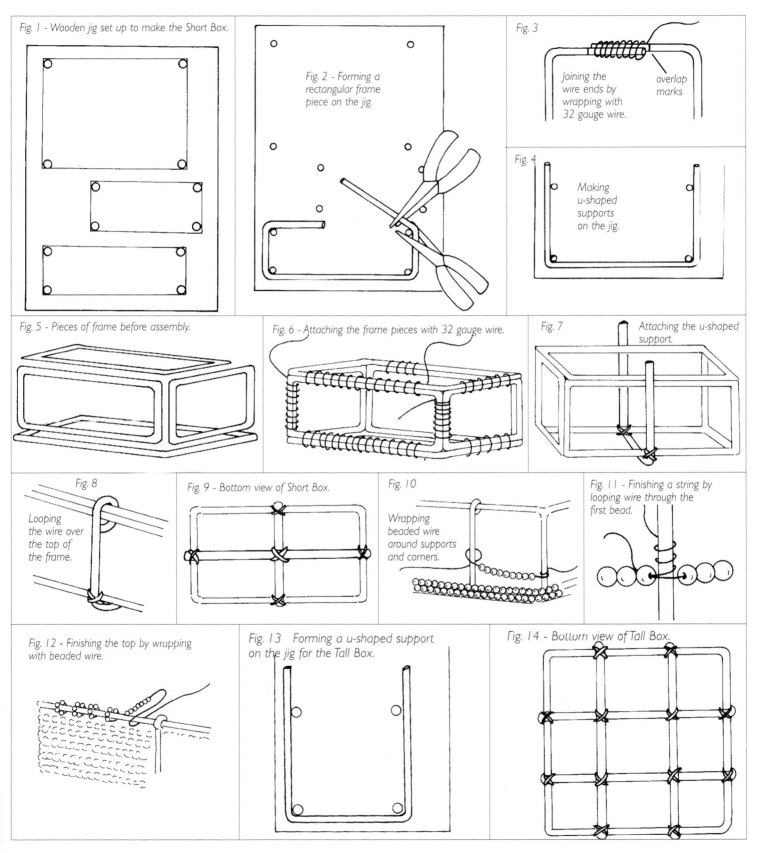

Fig. 1 - Wooden jig set up to make the Short Box.

Fig. 2 - Forming a rectangular frame piece on the jig.

Fig. 3

Joining the wire ends by wrapping with 32 gauge wire.

overlap marks

Fig. 4

Making u-shaped supports on the jig.

Fig. 5 - Pieces of frame before assembly.

Fig. 6 - Attaching the frame pieces with 32 gauge wire.

Fig. 7   Attaching the u-shaped support.

Fig. 8

Looping the wire over the top of the frame.

Fig. 9 - Bottom view of Short Box.

Fig. 10

Wrapping beaded wire around supports and corners.

Fig. 11 - Finishing a string by looping wire through the first bead.

Fig. 12 - Finishing the top by wrapping with beaded wire.

Fig. 13   Forming a u-shaped support on the jig for the Tall Box.

Fig. 14 - Bottom view of Tall Box.

continued from page 106

Add the Beads on the Bottom:

1. Secure one end of 32 gauge wire to the short side of the bottom frame. String green beads on the wire until you reach the support that crosses the bottom. Wrap the bare wire over and under the support wire and back over the top. See Fig. 10.
2. Continue adding beads until the opposite side of the box is reached. Wrap the loose end of the wire around the frame. Use glue to secure the end.
3. Continue this process until the bottom of the box is covered. If there is a gap in the beads over the support wires, glue the last bead from one side to the first

bead on the other with glue.

4. To cover the wire where the bottom joins the sides, secure a piece of 32 gauge wire to one corner of the bottom edge. String about 18" of beads on this wire. Place the beaded wire along the frame and wrap to secure with 32 gauge wire. When the corner where the strand was started is reached, add or subtract beads from the wire as needed and fill the space. Secure the beaded wire end by running it back through the first bead on the string and wrapping it around the frame. (Fig. 11.) Put a drop of glue on the end to hold it in place. Repeat this step to thoroughly cover the wire frame.

Add Beads on the Sides:

The sides are covered the same way as the bottom.

1. Secure the wire at a corner to begin each row and continue around the box until that corner is reached. Thread the wire back through the first bead when the row is complete. (Fig. 11)
2. To finish the box, thread 32 gauge wire with turquoise beads. Wrap them around the top of the box, thoroughly covering the top of the frame. See Fig. 12.
3. Secure the end of the string of beads to the box with 32 gauge wire. Seal all wire ends with glue. ❑

Tall Box
Pictured on page 105

SUPPLIES

32 gauge beading wire
16 gauge galvanized wire
12 oz. #8 lavender opaque glass seed beads
3 oz. #8 turquoise opaque glass seed beads
2 pair needlenose pliers
Roundnose pliers
Wire cutters
Jewelry glue
Marking pen
To make the wooden jig:
A piece of wood, 6" x 8", 1" thick.
1-1/2" box nails
Ruler
Pencil
Hammer

INSTRUCTIONS

The procedure for making the Tall Box is like that for making the Short Box. It may be helpful to you to consult the instructions and illustrations (Figs. 1-12) for the Short Box as you work, as the instructions for the Short Box are more detailed.

Make the Wooden Jig:

1. Make a jig.
2. Using the ruler, draw a 3" square near one corner of the piece of wood. Pound 1 nail into each corner of the square exactly where the lines cross, using 4 nails in all.
3. Draw a rectangle 3" x 4", leaving plenty of space between the rectangles, and pound nails in each corner as before.

Form Wire:

1. Cut 2 pieces of 16 gauge wire, each 16" long. Use these pieces to make two 3" squares on the jig. They are the top and bottom.
2. Cut 4 pieces of 16 gauge wire, each 17" long. Use these pieces to make four 3" x 4" rectangles on the jig. These are the sides of the box.
3. Cut four pieces of 16 gauge wire, each 15" long. Use the jig to make these into four U-shaped pieces 3" x 4". The bottom of the U will be the 3" side. See Fig. 13. These are the side and bottom supports.
4. Assemble the frame sides, bottom, and top as described in the Short Box instructions.
5. For the placement of the supports, mark every 1" on each side of the frame. Place 1 support over the bottom of the frame and line the sides up with one set of marks. Using a small amount of jewelry glue and 32 gauge wire, attach the supports to the frame. Repeat with the other supports.
6. Loop the wire over the top of the frame as shown in Fig. 8.

Add the Beads:

Add the beads, strung on wire, to the box, using lavender for the sides and bottom and turquoise for the top border. Follow the instructions given for the Short Box. ❑

Beaded Amber Lampshade

Instructions begin on page 108

BEADED AMBER

lampshade

A wire frame for this lampshade is formed around a terra cotta flowerpot. Use a candelabra-style lamp base with the shade.

By Pat McMahon

SUPPLIES

16 gauge galvanized wire
32 gauge beading wire
3 oz. burnt orange glass rocaille beads, #11
15 oz. amber glass rocaille beads, #10
1 #10 pushnut bolt retainer (from hardware store)
4" terra cotta rose pot
Jewelry glue
Marking pen
Ruler
Measuring tape
Masking tape
Pencil compass
2 pairs needlenose pliers
Roundnose pliers
Wire cutters

INSTRUCTIONS

Make Bulb Clamp:

1. Turn flower pot upside down on work surface. Use the measuring tape to divide the pot surface into six equal sections. Mark each section with a straight pencil line down the side of the pot. See Fig. 1.
2. Cut a piece of 16 gauge wire 12" and make a wire circle, forming the wire around the narrow end of the pot. Use the marking pen to mark where the wires overlap. Remove the circle from the pot.
3. Put a small amount of glue on the joint and press the ends together until the marks line up. Wrap this joint with 32 gauge wire.
4. Mark the circle with a marking pen, using the dividing marks on the pot as a guide. (Fig. 1)
5. Cut two 13" pieces of 16 gauge wire. At the center of each piece, form a u-shape 1-1/4" wide. Slide the pushnut bolt retainer over one wire (Fig. 2), then the other. Pull the wires through the retainer until the loops are 2-1/4" long.
6. Using needlenose pliers, bend wire across itself at the retainer and into a right angle over the top of the retainer. Bend the ends of the wires to form a circle that fits inside the wire circle you made in step #2. See Fig. 2. Wrap with 32 gauge wire to join the halves of the circle.
7. Curve the wire to fit inside the first circle and join with wire wraps. Set aside.

Make Frame:

1. Cut a piece of 16 gauge wire 15" long. Using rim of the pot, make a circle using the method in step #2 for the bulb clamp, above. Set aside.
2. Cut 6 pieces of 16 gauge wire, each 7" long and straighten them. These will be the ribs of the frame.
3. Using needlenose pliers, fold a right angle 1" from one end of each piece. Place the wire ribs on the pot on the marks you made in step #1 for the bulb clamp, above. Tape the wires in place to the pot. (Fig. 3) The wires will extend beyond the end of the pot and be forced out slightly by the weight of the pot.
4. Cut a piece of 16 gauge wire 15" long. Form this into a circle on top of the wires at the point where the rim begins. Wire and glue the circle shut as in step #2 for the bulb clamp, above.
5. Place a small amount of glue on each straight wire where the rim begins and place the wire circle over the frame. Attach with wraps of 32 gauge wire.
6. With a pencil compass, trace a circle 5-5/8" in diameter on a piece of paper to make a pattern. Cut a piece of 16 gauge wire 20" long. Form the wire into a circle on the pattern. Mark where the wires overlap. Set aside.
7. Turn the pot, with the wires still taped to it, right side up. Working one wire at a time, press the wires against the top of the pot. Holding the roundnose pliers on the wire at the edge of the pot, turn the wire away from the pot to make a small loop. See Fig. 4. Bend each wire gently away from the pot until each is 5/8" from the pot.
8. Thread the 5-5/8" wire circle you made in step #6 through the loops.
9. Line up the overlap marks on the circle. Glue and wrap wire to make circle.
10. Use the needlenose pliers to tighten the loops over the circle. (Fig. 4) Trim the excess wire from the loops with wire cutters.

Continued on page 112

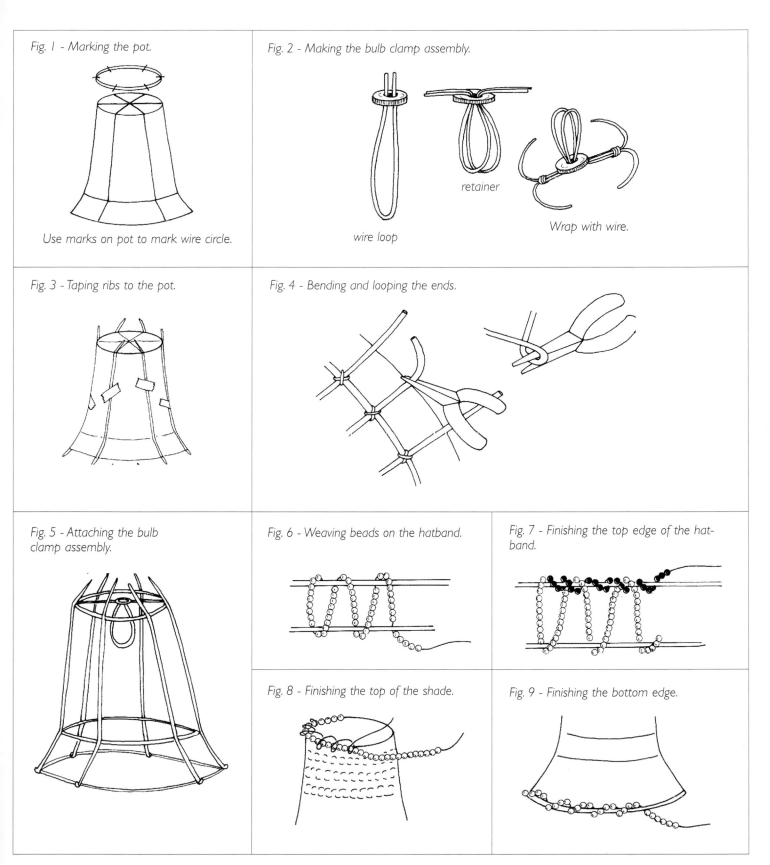

Fig. 1 - Marking the pot.

Use marks on pot to mark wire circle.

Fig. 2 - Making the bulb clamp assembly.

retainer

wire loop

Wrap with wire.

Fig. 3 - Taping ribs to the pot.

Fig. 4 - Bending and looping the ends.

Fig. 5 - Attaching the bulb clamp assembly.

Fig. 6 - Weaving beads on the hatband.

Fig. 7 - Finishing the top edge of the hatband.

Fig. 8 - Finishing the top of the shade.

Fig. 9 - Finishing the bottom edge.

Beaded Amber (cont.)

11. Remove the frame from the pot. Place the wire circle from "Make Frame," step #6 inside the frame and align it with the circle from step #4. Join the two circles with wraps of 32 gauge wire. Place a small amount of glue on the end of the 32 gauge wire to secure.

Assemble Frame:

1. Place the bulb clamp assembly inside the narrow end of the frame. (Fig. 5) Line up each rib with a mark on the small circle. Working one wire at a time, fold and loop the wire ribs over the bulb clamp assembly, using round-nose pliers. Use the needlenose pliers to tighten the loops around the circle. Trim excess wire with wire cutters.

2. Measure 5/8" up the side of the shade from the wire circles near the bottom and mark each rib. Cut a 14" long piece of 16 gauge wire and form a circle to fit over the marks. Mark the overlap point and glue and wrap with wire as before.

3. Put a small amount of glue on each rib at the mark. Align the circle over the marks and attach to the ribs with wraps of 32 gauge wire. This form the "hatband."

Attach Beads:

1. String burnt orange beads on lengths of 32 gauge wire. Weave over and under the hatband to cover. (Fig. 6) When you start or end a wire, wrap it securely to the frame and put a small amount of glue on the end.

2. Finish the top edge by threading 3 beads on a piece of 32 gauge wire. Wrap these beads over the top of the hatband and bring the bare wire to the front. Repeat, using 3 beads at a time, until the top of the hatband wire is covered. (Fig. 7)

3. Starting at the top of the hatband, cover the frame with amber beads strung on 32 gauge wire. Secure one end of the wire to the frame and string beads until you reach a rib. Wrap the bare wire over and under the rib and back over the top. Continue adding beads. Cover gaps over the ribs by gluing the last bead from one side to the first bead of the other. Each time a new wire is started or finished wrap it securely on the frame and put a small amount of glue on the end. Work around the shade toward the top of the frame.

4. At the top of the frame, string 10" of beads on a piece of 32 gauge wire. Place on the top edge of the frame and attach by wrapping with 32 gauge wire. It should conceal the top of the frame wire. See Fig. 8.

5. String beads to cover the bottom of the frame, working from the hatband to the lower edge.

6. At the bottom, string amber beads on 32 gauge wire and wrap around the bottom wire of the frame. (Fig. 9) Finish all wire ends with glue. ❏

SILVER SCROLLS

fruit bowl

This is a beautiful way to display fresh fruit. And it is easy to make your own fruit basket — simply make S-shaped wire pieces, secure together with wire wraps and you have a great looking bowl.

By Patty Cox

SUPPLIES

1/8" armature wire
24 gauge gold wire
Needlenose pliers

INSTRUCTIONS

1. Cut twelve 18" lengths armature wire. Bend each into an s-shape according to pattern.

2. Position two s-shapes together creating a heart-shape as shown. (See Pattern.) Secure s-shapes together with connecting wraps using 24 gauge gold wire.

3. Secure six heart-shapes together at with connecting wraps. Bring ends together, forming bowl sides. Secure ends with connecting wraps.

4. Cut 50" armature wire. Form into a large spiral for bowl bottom.

5. Secure outer ring of spiral to bases of heart-shapes with connecting wraps. ❏

*Pattern –
Enlarge @145%
for Actual Size.*

SCROLLS & JEWELS

light switch cover plate

Let nothing go undecorated – the creed of all creative people. A simple and inexpensive switch plate cover is decorated with wire and frosted marbles and changed into a piece of modern art.

By Patty Cox

Pattern – Actual Size

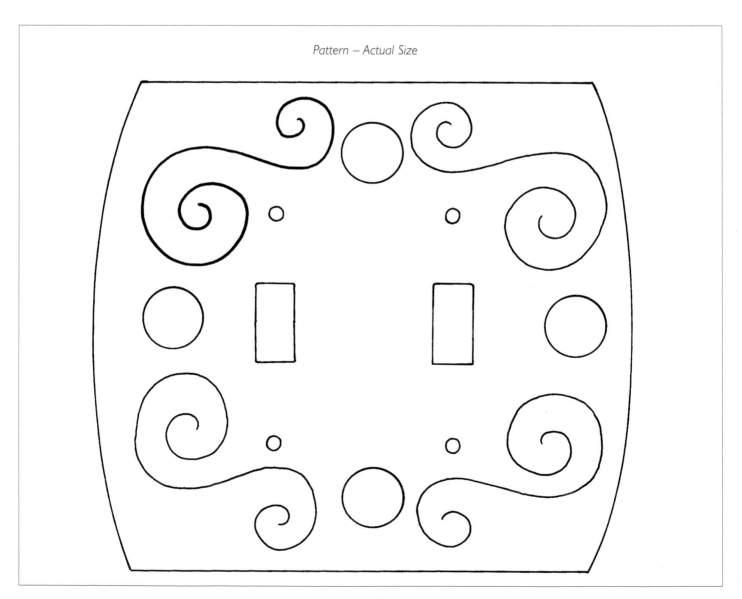

SUPPLIES

Thin solder wire
Brushed nickel double switch plate
    cover
4 frosted half marbles
Epoxy glue
Needlenose pliers

INSTRUCTIONS

1. Cut solder wire into four 7-1/2" pieces. Form each into an s-shape according to the pattern provided.
2. Glue s-shapes on switch plate in each corner using epoxy glue.
3. Glue a half marble in place between each s-shape. ❏

VINTAGE BEAUTY

lampshade

This shade looks like an antique, but you can make it today. It uses a ready-made frame. The frame can be any size or shape, but should have vertical ribs for wrapping the beads. This frame is 5" in diameter and 5" tall — if your frame is very large, you may need more beads than the amount specified. Use it with a candelabra-style base.

By Damema Spragens

SUPPLIES

1 gross assorted seed beads, color(s) of your choice
25 yd. spool of 26 gauge silver colored copper wire
26 gauge copper wire
26 gauge green wire
Lampshade frame
Jewelry glue
Wire cutters

INSTRUCTIONS

1. Cut a 2 yd. piece of wire. Measure 4" from one end. Wrap that end around a rib at the top of the frame. Secure the wire on the inside of the frame. (Fig. 1)
2. String on 1 yd. of beads.
3. Lay beaded wire horizontally across the next rib and wrap the beaded wire once around the rib, holding the seed beads in place. Pull the rest of the beaded wire around the rib. (Fig. 2)
4. Cover the frame with beads, wrapping the wire around the ribs of the frame. When you are within 3" of the end of the beaded wire, cut another 2-yd. piece of wire. Twist the wires together. Wrap the twist behind a rib. Continue stringing the beads and weaving.
5. When the shade is completely covered, take the last 3" of the last wire and wrap it around a rib on the bottom of the frame. Trim excess wire.
6. Wrap bottom of frame with copper wire to cover.
7. To make the scalloped trim on the bottom, string beads on silver wire. Loop between the ribs, securing with wire on the ribs on the inside of the frame.
8. Add additional loops by wrapping green wire on the bottom of the frame, stringing beads on the wire, and wrapping the end of the wire on the bottom of the frame.
9. Wrap the area where the bulb clamp joins the top of the frame with copper wire. Secure ends with drops of glue. ❑

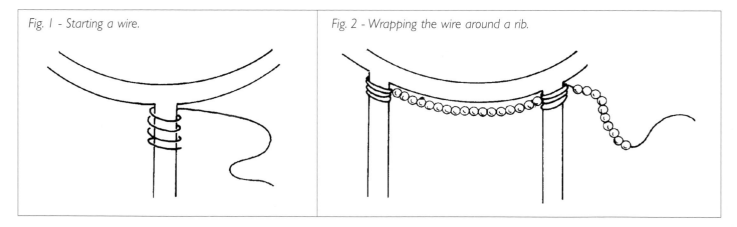

Fig. 1 - Starting a wire.

Fig. 2 - Wrapping the wire around a rib.

DIAMONDS & BUTTERFLIES

candle holder

An inexpensive clear glass votive holder is dressed up with leaf- and butterfly-shaped glass beads.

By Damema Spragens

SUPPLIES

Glass votive, 3-3/4" tall
20 round assorted glass beads, 6mm
8 green glass leaf beads, 10mm
4 black glass butterfly beads, 10mm
628 assorted seed beads, size 11
10 ft. 28 gauge copper wire
Thread

INSTRUCTIONS

1. Cut four 18" pieces of wire. Cut four 12" pieces of wire.
2. Fold an 18" piece of wire in half. Mark the half point with a piece of thread. String 42 seed beads on each end of the wire. (Fig. 1)
3. Place the ends of the wired seed beads together. Twist wires four to five times to create a ring of seed beads. (Fig. 2)
4. Take another 18" piece of wire and fold in half. Loop it at the bend on the ring of beads that you marked with thread. Twist five to seven times to secure. (Fig. 3)
5. Slip a leaf bead over each set of wires, pulling beads down to where the twists begin. Twist to secure. (Fig. 3)
6. Place votive upside down. Place wired ring of beads on the bottom of the votive. Let both sets of wires hang down the sides of the glass. (Fig. 3) Bend each set of wires over the rim of the glass so they lie flat on the sides of the votive. Turn the votive right side up.

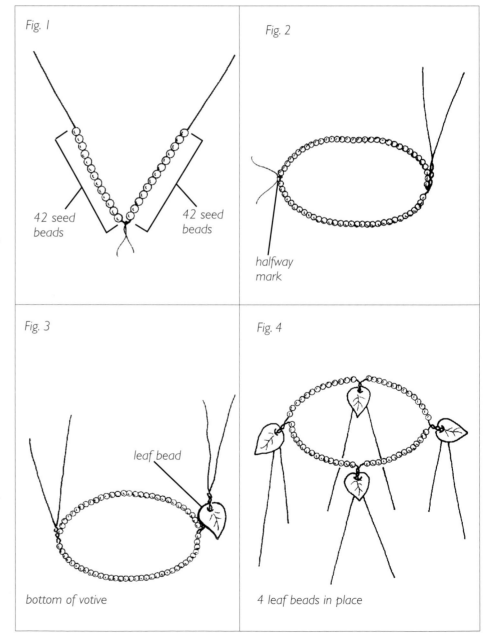

Fig. 1 — 42 seed beads · 42 seed beads

Fig. 2 — halfway mark

Fig. 3 — leaf bead / bottom of votive

Fig. 4 — 4 leaf beads in place

7. Fold another 18" piece of wire in half. Count 21 seed beads from one set of wires. Place wire at fold around the ring of seed beads between the twenty-first and twenty-second beads. Twist 5-7 times to secure. (Twists should be equal in length to those of other wires.) (Fig. 4)

8. Slip a leaf bead over the pair of wires. Pull down to the spot were the twist begins. Twist 3-4 times to secure. (Fig. 4)

9. Repeat with the remaining 18" piece of wire. (Fig. 4)

10. Separate each pair of wires and string 28 seed beads on each piece of wire. Fold wires horizontally. Twist where wires meet to form a circle of beads around the sides of the votive near the bottom.

11. Take the four 12" pieces of wire. Fold in half and twist to attach above each leaf on the circle of beads near the bottom.

12. Separate the pairs of wires and string 14 seed beads on each piece of wire above the twist. Twist adjacent wires together 3-4 times to secure and form triangle shapes.

13. Slide a butterfly, leaf, or 6mm bead over the twisted wire, selecting beads randomly.

14. Separate the pairs of wire and string 14 more seed beads on each piece of wire. Twist and secure with a butterfly, leaf, or 6mm bead.

15. String 5 seed beads and top with remaining leaf beads or 6mm beads.

16. Twist top of wires for 1" to secure. Make a loop with twisted wires and cut off excess. Bend over top edge of votive to secure. ❑

Holidays

Decorations for tree and tabletop make up the projects in this section. They're colorful and fun to make and can be used year after year.

Pictured right: Tabletop Forest Beaded Trees.

TABLETOP FOREST

beaded trees

Cover foam cones with paint and sparkly beads to create a wonderland forest of trees.
These make great holiday table centerpieces.

By Jennifer Jacob

SUPPLIES

3 plastic foam cones, 4" x 9"
Double-sticky tape, 1" and 1/4" widths
Tiny holeless beads, green
Green and gold seed beads and gold
    bugle beads
A few gold beads, 3mm
Gold straight pins
3 wooden balls with flat bottoms - two
    1-1/2", one 1"
Acrylic craft paint - red
Paint brush
Serrated saw or steak knife
Scissors
Shoebox lids, 1 for each color of beads
Sandpaper

INSTRUCTIONS

1. Cut the cones down to 3", 6", and 9" heights with a serrated saw or steak knife. Sand the bottoms smooth so they will stand up straight.
2. Cover the cones with strips of double-sticky tape. Don't overlap the strips, and keep them as flat as possible. Trim tape with scissors as needed.
3. Pour the tiny green beads in a shoebox lid. Remove the backing from the tape and roll the cones in the beads, pressing them in the beads until they are completely covered. Lift.
4. Apply double-sticky tape in stripes or spirals to the cones, using photo as a guide for placement. Remove the backing from the tape and roll the cones in a mixture of green seed beads, gold seed beads, and gold bugle beads. Press the beads on the tape until the tape is covered. Shake off excess over the box lid.
5. Paint wooden balls with red paint. Let dry.
6. Put glue on the flat bottoms of the wooden balls. Position the balls on top of the trees, placing the 1" ball on the smallest tree. Let dry.
7. *Option:* Add 3mm gold beads to some of the trees, using gold straight pins to hold them. ❏

SUGAR PLUMS

tree ornaments

Tiny holeless beads and double-sticky tape make it easy to create these sparkling decorations for your tree.

By Jennifer Jacob

SUPPLIES

3 plastic foam balls, 2" diameter
Double-sticky tape, 1/4" wide
Gold wire-edge ribbon, 1/8" wide
Burgundy wire-edge ribbon, 1/2" wide
White craft glue
Straight pins
Shoebox lids (for holding the beads)
Dollmaker's needle
Scissors

INSTRUCTIONS

1. Run the 1/8" ribbon through the ball with a dollmaker's needle and return on the same path to make the hanger. Tie the ends of the ribbon together and trim the tails. Pull the loop so the knot is flush with the ball. Glue both ends of the ribbon to the ball. Allow to dry completely.

2. Cover the ball with double-sticky tape. Make sure the strips lie flat and don't overlap. Some snipping with scissors may be necessary. Note: You can use the tape to make designs, such as stripes or spirals.

3. Pour the tiny beads in a shoebox lid. Peel the backing paper off the tape. Note: If you are planning to use more than one color of beads, leave the backing paper on in the area where the second color will be placed. Roll the ball in the beads until the exposed tape is covered. Lift. If you're using a second bead color, remove the backing paper from the remaining tape. Pour the beads in another shoe box lid. Roll the ornament in the beads until the tape is covered. Lift.

4. *Option:* Apply more tape over the tiny beads. Remove backing paper. Roll in a mixture of white and gold seed beads and gold bugle beads.

5. Decorate the ornaments with bows of wire-edge ribbon and secure with straight pins. You can also wrap the balls with ribbon before attaching a bow. ❑

SPIRAL TREE

holiday decoration

This tabletop tree is easy to store, so you can use it year after year. It is just the right touch to brighten an entry table or to decorate your holiday dining table.

By Patty Cox

SUPPLIES

2 yds. 1/4" armature wire
24 gauge gold wire
24 gauge silver wire
35 round beads, 3/8" - various colors
Gold head pins
Jewelry glue
Toothpick
Pliers
Roundnose pliers

INSTRUCTIONS

1. Hold end of armature wire with pliers. Tightly coil wire. End with a smaller coil (about 3-1/2").
2. Secure small ending coil with a connecting wrap of 24 gauge wire.
3. Open coil, forming tree to desired height.
4. Insert a head pin through a round bead. Bend head pin wire around a spiral on tree. Dot clear epoxy glue on wire with a toothpick to secure bead in place on tree.
5. To make icicles, spiral 24 gauge wire around roundnose pliers. Bend end of wire around a spiral on tree. Dot clear epoxy glue on wire to secure icicle in position. ❏

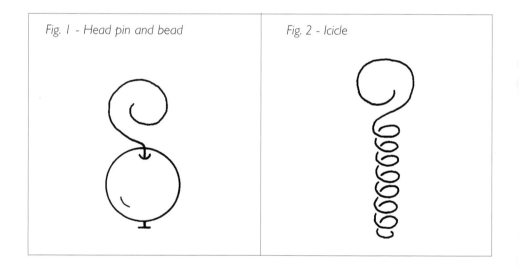

Fig. 1 - Head pin and bead

Fig. 2 - Icicle

BEADED FRUIT

place card holders

These beaded fruit make colorful table decorations for a beautiful holiday dining table.

By Jennifer Jacob

SUPPLIES

Foam or plastic fruits, 1-1/2-2" tall
Gold split rings, 1", 1 for each fruit
1/2" washers, one for each fruit
(You can also use penny coins.)
Florist's wire
Green wire-edge ribbon, 1/2" wide
Translucent seed beads in colors to
match the fruit
Heavy duty thread in colors to match
the beads
Glue gun and glue sticks
Beading needles

INSTRUCTIONS

1. Remove the stem from fruit.
2. Cut a piece of florist's wire 3" long. Double and twist around the break in the split ring.
3. Stick the wire in the stem hole. Hot glue the ring upright to secure.
4. Thread a beading needle with double thread and knot the end, using a piece of thread as long as you can work with comfortably. String the beads, leaving about 12" of thread at the needle end.
5. Glue the washer (or a penny) to the bottom of the fruit to stabilize it. Place the end of the threaded beads into the glue around the washer and wrap them in a spiral around the fruit, securing with glue every 1/2". Wet your fingers to press the beads into the glue to prevent the glue from making messy strings.
6. When you reach the top of the piece of fruit, run the beads through the

bottom of the split ring to help secure it. If your thread runs out before you reach the top, tie off the thread and start a new string of beads.
7. Tie off your last bead and secure it with glue. Take care not to leave a gap in the beads on the fruit. ❑

Metric Conversion Chart

Inches to Millimeters and Centimeters

Inches	MM	CM
1/8	3	.3
1/4	6	.6
3/8	10	1.0
1/2	13	1.3
5/8	16	1.6
3/4	19	1.9
7/8	22	2.2
1	25	2.5
1-1/4	32	3.2
1-1/2	38	3.8
1-3/4	44	4.4
2	51	5.1
3	76	7.6
4	102	10.2
5	127	12.7
6	152	15.2
7	178	17.8
8	203	20.3
9	229	22.9
10	254	25.4
11	279	27.9
12	305	30.5

Yards to Meters

Yards	Meters
1/8	.11
1/4	.23
3/8	.34
1/2	.46
5/8	.57
3/4	.69
7/8	.80
1	.91
2	1.83
3	2.74
4	3.66
5	4.57
6	5.49
7	6.40
8	7.32
9	8.23
10	9.14

Index

Index